The
Storm

*Stories to help you
overcome your
darkest days.*

By Jen Guidry

A wholly owned subsidiary of **TBN**

The Storm

Trilogy Christian Publishers A Wholly Owned Subsidiary of Trinity Broadcasting Network

2442 Michelle Drive Tustin, CA 92780

For information about special discounts for bulk purchases, please contact Trilogy Christian Publishing.

Manufactured in the United States of America

10 9 8 7 6 5 4 3 2 1

Library of Congress Cataloging-in-Publication Data is available.

ISBN: 978-1-63769-372-8

E-ISBN: 978-1-63769-373-5

To my precious husband, Michael, who has been right by my side. Thank you for loving me.

Also, a special thank you to my work team. Mary Moore, Robert Meagher, Ryan Fay, and Rose Hernandez, I could not have written this book without you holding down the fort while I was sick. Without your help, this would not have been possible.

Thank you to Debbie Mann, who has always given me honest feedback and great advice.

Finally, thank You, Jesus, for Your inspiration and strength.

Table of Contents

Table of Contents

Prologue

This is not your typical Christian Book. It's for real life. It is written the way I think… and it can sometimes be a little raw. These are stories--mostly of my own--that I compiled to help you through a major life change. You know, like when you just get some bad or devastating news or a not-so-great medical diagnosis.

Maybe you're having a bad day or a series of bad days! This book is for you. It's meant to make you laugh, think, pray, and to integrate into your daily life. Let me show you how God can take your darkest days and use them for good. It may sound impossible right now, but read on and see.

I titled this book *The Storm* because storms are mighty and powerful. They sometimes come when you're not expecting them, and they have the ability to radically transform everything they touch. Sometimes things aren't the same after storms, and that is OKAY. Storms change things… that is what they do. The great thing about them is this: they don't last forever.

Storms cleanse us. They shake the loose branches and dead limbs off of us to make room for future growth. Storms might come with the apparent initial thought of, *wow, this really sucks,* but in the end, you will be a better person--if you figure out how to respond to them. You will find reason in them. Comfort in them. Faith in them. You will use them for good and to understand the meaning of the storm you're going through right now.

This book contains my stories and lessons written with an open heart and complete transparency. As I compiled what I wanted to share with you, it was apparent that four major "Life Themes" emerged, and I organized my writings into those themes, which became the 4 parts of this book:

Part I: Be Still, This Is What Matters

Part II: Your Past and Your Future

Part 3: Gratitude

Part 4: Overcoming

At the end of each part, there is space for you to journal your own thoughts and prayers. Completing these tasks will be an important part of your healing and restoration. You don't have to do them all at once. Just take your time and read and think. Come back to things. My hope is that they bring you great peace and understanding of whatever you are going through right now.

This book is meant to be read a day at a time (or more if you like!), so take your time.

Prologue

As they sailed across, Jesus settled down for a nap. But soon a fierce storm came down on the lake. The boat was filling with water, and they were in real danger. The disciples went and woke him up, shouting, "Master, Master, we're going to drown!" When Jesus woke up, he rebuked the wind and the raging waves. Suddenly the storm stopped, and all was calm. Then he asked them, "Where is your faith?" The disciples were terrified and amazed. "Who is this man?" they asked each other. "When he gives a command, even the wind and waves obey him!"

— LUKE 8:23-25, NLT

PART 1:

Be Still, This Is What Matters

Chapter 1: The Storm

Mondays. *Ugh*. Those were the toughest days of the week. So many phone calls came in along with countless emails and text messages. The phone became a never-ending "ding-fest," delivering notifications of the messages flying in. Sometimes, it seemed impossible to get all of my work done.

Over two hundred emails. Twenty plus text messages, and now eight voicemails. *It is not even 10:00 a.m. Geesh!* I would say to myself. I would already be anxious and stressed out, even though my day hadn't even officially started.

One Monday morning, I went to the doctors because I was having trouble breathing. I was actually convinced that I had COVID-19. While I waited to be seen, I was checking my work email as I sat on the examination table in a hospital gown. The doctor came in and delivered the bad news. *Crap*, I thought. *Not again*. I knew what I was in for. The weakness, the pain, the recovery...

A single tear rolled down my right cheek as I took a breath in. I sighed.

My heart was failing, and I had "massive" clots in both of my lungs. I could die. If I would have waited one more day, I would have. That was a lot to take in on a Monday.

I had to make a decision: accept the prognosis and surrender to my circumstances, or be defeated. Was I to be pissed off, bitter, and anxious? Have a pity party for myself? Be a victim?

Or did I want to use my abilities to get a little creative with healing this time? Explore the positive side of my circumstances? Make the best of them?

The doctor made his opinion clear: "It is going to take time to heal from this, and for now, you have to rest. Your life depends on it."

Time--my past and future, which had whirled around me just a few eye-blinks earlier--came to an abrupt halt. Nothing else concerned me more than the present situation. *Maybe God is trying to tell me something*, I thought. *Slow down. Find Me. Seek Me. Be dependent on Me.*

"I already know this stuff!" I whispered.

"But do you?" God said.

The constant dinging of my phone stopped mattering. The fretful thoughts that I had just moments ago about all of the emails and voicemails and texts to return meant nothing to me. Not one other thing mattered except for the moment I was in right then. My body was fighting to keep functioning. To stay alive.

Nothing. Else. Mattered.

I immediately felt a ton of stress being lifted, and it felt weird. I would've thought that it would be the opposite. I actually giggled a little at this realization, and the smile stayed on my face for quite some time.

Time stopped, and stillness became my superpower.

The past and the future were insignificant. Only now mattered.

I used time wisely. After never taking significant time off of work before, I found it agreeable, actually. It ended up being four months. I healed my body and quieted my mind for the first time in twenty years. The things that used to stress me out didn't have that hold on me anymore. Sweet, sweet freedom.

It was fascinating to witness the ideas and the thoughts that came into my mind. Words. Purpose. Questions. Appreciation. Gratitude. Love. Peace. I felt more.

I felt that God came closer to me and put His arm around me. He spoke to me. Loud and clear.

"This... now THIS is what I want you to do, my dear child. This is what I want from you and what you have been missing, but you were too busy to see. I kept on giving you heart tugs and some gentle nudges. I know you felt them, you just didn't know what to do with them. This is what I want you to do, and you would not pause long enough to grasp my messages. So... I slowed you down.

"In my defense though, I did spend the last ten years preparing your body for this change so that you would survive.

Now here we are. Enjoy and fulfill YOUR purpose."

"Okay, God. I am listening," I said.

Surrender to *The Storm*.

And now, readers, I ask you to do the same thing. Realize that the most important thing is the thing that you are doing right now. Maybe you're going through a major setback right now. You feel defeated. The life that "was" just yesterday is not the same today. It is so different. You are scared.

"Now what?" you say. In moments when everything has changed, those changes can unnerve you. Don't let that happen.

Realize that not one human thing lasts forever, including what you're going through right now. It may not seem like it, but this too shall pass. The question is, what are you gonna do about it?

Open your heart to its lessons. There is a reason for all of this. Now is the time to figure it out.

> And the God of all grace, who called you to his eternal glory in Christ, after you have suffered a little while, will himself restore you and make you strong, firm and steadfast.
>
> **— 1 PETER 5:10, NIV**

> Therefore, since we have been justified through faith, we[a] have peace with God through our Lord

The Storm

Jesus Christ, through whom we have gained access by faith into this grace in which we now stand. And we boast in the hope of the glory of God. Not only so, but we also glory in our sufferings, because we know that suffering produces perseverance; perseverance, character; and character, hope. And hope does not put us to shame, because God's love has been poured out into our hearts through the Holy Spirit, who has been given to us.

— **ROMANS 5:1-5, NIV**

Chapter 2: In the Darkest Places - A Prayer

It has been a while, God, since I have been at this place. You tell me to "trust You" and that everything will be "okay." I will see... "soon," you say.

There are things that I can only see in my stillness and when I rest my weary body. The person You want me to be, the person I was MADE to be--she's there, waiting for me to be ready. I know that I can never be satisfied with only thinking about You and knowing You intrinsically. When I search for You, I will know You practically and intimately. There's a difference. I can feel it.

You tell me that I can't have a testimony unless there's a test. I get it. I now have a lot of dang testimonies, God. A LOT. I will share them wisely, with others so they know the power that You have to turn what is meant for harm into good.

I'm scared right now, God. I need You to wrap Your arms around me and provide me with Your comfort. The kind only You can give. When I whisper Your name so softly, please come stand next to me. Protect me with Your armor as I prepare for the battle ahead. I feel so weak right now, and my body is tired. I need Your strength, Lord. The kind only You can give. Amen

Chapter 3:
Everything or Nothing

Which would you rather have:

A miracle or the ordinary?

Unfailing love or conditional love?

Supernatural or normal?

Freedom or slavery?

Forgiveness or punishment?

Hope or despair?

Truth or lies?

Grace or judgment?

Unchanging and absolute promises or relative truth?

Victory or defeat?

Strength when weary or frailty?

Plans to prosper or plans for failure?

The knowledge that you are never alone or isolation?

Rest or restlessness?

Abundant blessings or affliction?

Light or darkness?

Eternal life or damnation?

Wisdom or foolishness?

Everything or nothing?

The list of polar opposite words above each represent two very different worlds in which we can live. I have lived in both. Lots of people have.

I like the "everything" world better. I can do all things through Christ who strengthens me. When you have a relationship with God and choose the everything life, something amazing happens. You get a very special and supernatural strength that continues to grow within you. Your life changes from the inside-out. It is gradual at first, but one day you will wake up and find that the "old you" is gone--replaced with a much better, shinier version of yourself. You'll see it. Others will too. When you realize the power that you have with God in your life, extraordinary things happen.

Apart from God, you can do nothing. Sure, you can live your life as a pretty decent person. Then what? What's the purpose? The point? What are you living FOR actually?

Without God, I can do nothing. With God, I can do everything. It really is that simple.

Which life do you choose?

> Yes, I am the vine; you are the branches. Those who remain in me, and I in them, will produce much

Everything or Nothing

fruit. For apart from me you can do nothing.

— JOHN 15:5, NLT

For I can do everything through Christ, who gives me strength.

— PHIL 4:13, NLT

Chapter 4:
Finding Peace

Amidst everything going on all around us, we have the ability to find peace. Peace amongst the chaos and the clammer. Look for the good that comes through pain and trouble, and you'll realize that understanding just isn't going to work when you're in a storm... only trust and faith will get you through.

Having inner peace calms the whirlwind that rotates around you like your own personal tornado. I know you know what I'm talking about--you're probably feeling it right now, right? All of these events, the news, your worries, your fears, anxiety... all going 1000 miles per hour around you, much like a tornado. You take a step, and the storm follows you, rotating so quickly you can't even keep up... too many things spinning.

Imagine this: having peace turns that whirlwind into a comfortable breeze on a sunny day that warms you and brings a smile to your face--despite the unpleasant experiences going on all around you. Your anxieties are calmed, and your mind gets cleared. Peace.

Right now, it's hard to look for the good coming out of

our days... hours... minutes... because of all the negativity often thrust into our lives.

Things are changing, and we have two choices:

1) Trust God and have that peace in your heart and mind that, in the end, everything is going to be okay, OR

2) Have your own personal tornado.

In both instances, the stimulus is the same, and the reality of what is going on in the world is the same... but it's up to you to choose your reaction to it. That's the only thing that we can control--our response. Will it be one of trust? Or adding to the chaos?

> I have told you these things, so that in me you may have peace. In this world you will have trouble. But take heart! I have overcome the world.
>
> — JOHN 16:33, NIV

> Glory to God in the highest heaven, and on earth peace to those on whom his favor rests.
>
> — LUKE 2:14, NIV

Chapter 5: Lessons from a Paint by Number

One thing I've been doing to keep myself busy during my downtime is completing a good old-fashioned paint by number. They're making a comeback, ya know! My mom reminded me that my grandparents used to have them in their house when I was young, but those were mostly of clowns and mountains. Let's just say though, paint by numbers have come a long way in forty years.

As I first took my canvas out of the package and carefully unrolled it, I admit that I got overwhelmed. My eyes bulged a little as they tried to make out the approximately eighty-six trillion individual spaces to paint in with numbers that you might need a magnifying glass to see. I actually gave the project a second thought because it looked too daunting and tedious for me to complete. But I tackled it anyway.

I prepared my canvas. Chose an area to start and began working on it. Little teeny number by number. One at a time. I loved every second of it. I was fully focused on my task at hand. I was making brush strokes and filling in empty spaces in order to work towards my finished masterpiece. Sometimes the paint placement didn't make any sense to me, but I knew my concern didn't matter. It would all come together in the end when it was finished. Then, I would see. It was going to be amazing.

On day two, as I had begun to paint, I had a revelation that made me pause, and I haven't been able to get it out of my head since (this is how I always know I am supposed to do something, when it won't go away).

Here's the thing. My paint by number is a great metaphor for what God does in our lives. Work with me here. Imagine that we're the canvas, and God is the painter. He laid out our lives ahead of us (which are the different numbers to be filled in). We see the eighty-six trillion numbers. God sees where the paint--the experiences, trials, joys, sorrows, suffering, love, laughter, relationships, tears, mistakes, faith, understanding, hope, and trust--is going to go. He sees the bigger picture, looking at it from a view that we can't see from our viewpoint.

He sees the grace--where we see the space. He sees the *piece de resistance* while we see number twelve paint--which is suffering. He knows that after suffering, there will come number fourteen paint--joy. I wish we could see that with Him, but our view is too limited.

Color by color, number by number, we become who we are through Him.

Sometimes He completes huge amounts of one paint or large clusters of paint at what will seem like all at one time.

Lessons from a Paint by Number

The color is patterned throughout our canvas with no particular rhyme or reason, it seems to us. We have to trust that the great artist knows what He is doing. I know that we can't see it, but we have to remember that we are not God. We're looking at the paint on our canvases from ground level.

As time progresses, we experience more trials, more joy, more sorrow, and we wonder why. Why did You let this happen, Lord? I am hurting right now. Or, thank You, God, for all of my blessings. I can't believe this happened! Or, thank God THAT is over!

And He replies, "My dear child, wait until you see what I see. One day you will. You are only seeing it from up-close. I see it from heaven."

The Storm

And one day we do. We get to see ourselves as God created us to be. We come to realize that all of the trials, the love, laughter, tears, suffering, and joy made us into this spectacular masterpiece. We will understand that we had to go through all those things so that we could have this AMAZING testimony about what He can do in our lives. Every single paint stroke was made for a reason. There was a plan.

I hope you let Him do it--paint your picture. I hope you don't throw away your valuable showpiece because you don't understand what had to go into it to making it. I know we can't always see the bigger picture. We aren't supposed to. That is where trust and faith come in.

There is a reason.

Things might not have gone the way YOU wanted, and that is OKAY. Storms will come out better, even when you can't see it right away. You are being prepared. You are being pruned, painted over by the greatest artist that has existed since the beginning and will never end. The King of Kings, The Almighty, The Holy One, The Great Shepherd, The Light of the World, and The Author and Perfecter of our faith is painting YOUR picture. My picture. He knows what He is doing. Promise.

We do this by keeping our eyes on Jesus, the champion who initiates and perfects our faith. Because of the joy awaiting him, he endured the cross, disregarding shame. Now he is seated in the place of honor besides God's throne.

— HEBREWS 12:2, NIV

"I am the Alpha and the Omega, the First and the Last, the Beginning and the End."

— REVELATIONS 22:13, NIV

Chapter 6: Why Does God Allow Suffering?

Why does He? Why would He allow such tragedy?

I used to struggle with this. I admit it. Suffering sucks. Why would such a great God let His children suffer?

Before I can give you my answer to that question, there is some background that needs to be covered.

Free will: God has given us the choice to love Him or not. To be close to Him or not. To ask for forgiveness or not. Either way, it's OUR choice. He is with us always, regardless.

Good and evil: If we didn't have evil, we would not have good. All of us have sinned and all of us have some evil in us, even if we don't care to admit it. I know I do! If we didn't have good and evil, we would not have absolute truth--right and wrong. It would just be us "perfect, good" people in the world with nothing to strive for... no consequences... no true standard of right and wrong.

When we look at things we don't like, we make the mistake of thinking we know more than God does because the presence of evil doesn't fit into our minds. We have a limited perspective, He does not. He doesn't see things like humans do, and He doesn't think like we do. He's God. We are not.

We can't use our limited logic to understand all that He does.

When we try and wrap our heads around, "Why God allows suffering," the answer is simpler than you think, but you might not like the answer.

God dwells in eternity. Forever. Always. The Beginning and the End. There is no time or space or dimension where He is not present. In contrast, our fallen world sure does not dwell in eternity. Not even close. This world is temporary. Heaven is eternity. The time we have on earth is NOTHING compared to eternity.

God's primary objective is to love and be loved in return (which, I also believe that we humans are hardcoded to want the same exact thing in our lives) by His children... us.

God tells us time and time again that suffering in this world is temporary compared to eternity with Him. He uses the pain, suffering, trials, and sadness of this world to prepare us for forever with Him. Our momentary time on earth is nothing compared to eternity. I know I keep saying that...

The cool thing is this: suffering is going to happen, but God also promises us that He has a plan for everything to work out at the end. Best example that I can think of right now: Jesus. He died for our redemption. Good from bad. Always. Even if we can't readily see it or make "human" sense of it.

We have to stop looking at things from OUR limited human point-of-view and remember that God looks at things from eternity.

All I know is this: when you accept God into your life, EVERYTHING changes. You change from the inside-out, and nothing is the same. THAT is how I know.

> For our light and momentary troubles are achieving for us an eternal glory that far outweighs them all.
>
> — 2 CORINTHIANS 4:17, NIV

> I consider that our present sufferings are not worth comparing with the glory that will be revealed in us.
>
> — ROMANS 8:18, NIV

Chapter 7: I Thought That I Was Having a Bad Day

On a bright and early Monday morning, I was headed up to Dallas to our corporate office for some meetings. I was having "one of those mornings." I didn't get to work out because someone (which is me) booked a 7:30 a.m. flight! I called an Uber, and when I got in the car, I realized I forgot my necklace on the counter. *Dang.* I was slightly perturbed that I was B 29 instead of A 1-15 on Southwest. When I got to the airport, I realized I had a giant hole in the side of my skirt, and my undies were free to be seen by all. Free show! I found myself grumbling about the most stupid crap, whereas now as I write this, I laugh at how ridiculous I was that morning.

Anyway, here was where God stepped in and smacked me upside the head... again. For like the 1039483287th time.

After I changed my skirt, I was at the gate, and someone I hadn't seen for a while flagged me down. We started chit-chatting. I could tell he was sad. He shared that he was going through a very long divorce and was heading back home to help take care of his very, very ill father who was near the end of his life in hospice. I gave him a hug, and he walked away.

When he left to go to his gate, I prayed for him and his family. Not five minutes later, I got a text from another friend of mine telling me that he was heading to Oklahoma because his father had just passed away in the night.

Stop whatever you are doing and go hug your dad if he is around!

And here I was, complaining about my "first world problems" that were ridiculous and meaningless. *Okay God, I get it.*

The point is this: we get caught up in our own little worlds. We worry about stuff that just doesn't freakin' matter--while there are people all around us suffering with REAL issues. Way worse than not getting A1-15 on Southwest. I think sometimes God gives us reminders of how important it is to just remain in Him. Small and big stuff, He is there with us. If we acknowledge Him.

I have learned through the years that no matter what we THINK we are suffering with, someone else has it worse. Someone has more heartache. Worse health. Less food. Less money. More violence. Worse issues.

This knowledge taught me to be more patient with people, especially when they apparently do bad or rude things to me, because I have learned that 99.99999999% of the time, it has NOTHING to do with me at all. They have something else going on in their life. Heartache. Illness. Sadness. Anxiety. Bitterness. Fatigue. Stress.

I don't get mad anymore when people cut me off on the road because I was once that person racing down the freeway at ninety miles per hour, tailgating. Why? Because my stepdad was just rushed to the hospital, and I needed to be there. Remember that next time you get mad at someone on the road. Maybe they have an emergency. Just get the heck out of the way. Maybe they are just a jerk. You don't know. Remember it's not about YOU, it's about them.

Most of the time, it's difficult not to sweat that "small stuff."

When I feel myself starting to do this, I have retrained myself to think about how freakin' blessed I am. Sometimes, though, God has to remind me as He did on Monday. I think about all that I have to be thankful for in my life. Then the other stuff doesn't matter. I also really try and have compassion for those that I meet or see or encounter every day. We aren't here to judge people--we're supposed to love them. Even the ones you don't want to love.

For our light and momentary troubles are achieving for us an eternal glory that far outweighs them all. So we fix our eyes not on what is seen, but on what is unseen, since what is seen is temporary, but

The Storm

what is unseen is eternal.

— 2 CORINTHIANS 4:17-18, NIV

Search me, God, and know my heart; test me and know my anxious thoughts.

— PSALM 139:23, NIV

Chapter 8: The Story of the Nose Bite and the Prayer

It is hard for me to believe sometimes that I was in an abusive relationship. A bad one. It was a dude that came from a "good family," but he wasn't good. By the time I realized what I had gotten into, it was too late, I was already sucked into love and stupid as can be. Love was truly blind. He was horribly verbally abusive to me, and then one day it became physical.

The jerk bit my nose in a confrontation. A deep bite. They could not stitch my nose because it was a human bite, so I had to walk around with a taped nose, all huge and red for several weeks. My scar is still visible despite the multiple times of getting it lasered. Now, it serves as a reminder to me to be careful and to know the red flags that I had chosen to ignore way back then.

I am a strong woman, very strong. I sometimes shake my head when I think of back then and wonder how I got myself into that mess. It was crazy. It was scary. Now, I use it as a learning tool of the perennial reminder of what NOT to do. Learn from me, young people!

I tell you this because it's a back story on what has become one of the greatest moments in my life:

God talking to me again, and me listening.

During that time, my stepfather was very ill. He had been in and out of the hospital many, many times. That man endured so much, and he fought so hard. It was a very difficult time for our family. For a while, he even took up pretty much permanent residence at my house so that I could help my mom.

Marv was one of the best people I know. He was a total smarty pants. He loved my mother deeply, and he worked hard. He was a loyal and all around just a great dude. He used to help me write papers at 2 a.m. the day before they were due while I was in college (I just loved this about him) because I would always wait until the last minute. He was just an amazing man.

He and I used to have "God talks" a lot because he SAID that he did not believe in God, but I had figured out what it really was--that he was mad at God for some reason. He and I would playfully argue back and forth about this quite a bit.

I always told him that if I was wrong, it was not a big deal, but if HE was wrong, then it was...

Fast forward to a Monday morning while he was in the hospital for the 5,646,346 time. I had a dream where God told me that I had to write a prayer to lead Marv to Him. Oh, and I had to get up right then to do it.

The Story of the Nose Bite and the Prayer

So, I did. I woke up super early and wrote the prayer, which I shared with you at the end of this chapter. I sped my butt down to the hospital, got there around 7:00 a.m., walked into his room, and shut the door.

When I walked in, Marv was surprised to see me. He looked at me because I was smiling and said, "Jen, how are you always so happy? How can you be smiling when THAT just happened to you?" He was talking about my nose. "You and I, Jen… we always seem to get the bad breaks. Yet you are happy. How?"

"My relationship with God. My life with Him in it is so much better than when I was without. He changes you from the inside out," I said. We talked for a bit and laughed. I will never forget his smile (more like a smirk) as we joked about all of the crazy stuff that had happened over the years.

Then I told him about my dream and the prayer. I asked him if he would repeat it after me as I read it to him.

He just shook his head and said, "Okay, Jen. I am ready…"

As I write this, I'm crying because it was so beautiful and such a very tender moment in my life. The moments are like snapshots in my memory that I hope never goes away.

We read the prayer together. We were both bawling with tears. I stayed a little while longer to visit him, and then I went to work.

Marv passed away shortly after that.

I thank God often for that dream--for that moment--and I think now, *Imagine if I had not listened.*

God speaks to us. He really does. Most times, we don't hear Him because we're too busy worrying about things or too busy with our lives. Please pause long enough to listen to Him. He speaks to us in the quiet of the morning or in our dreams--by coincidences or moments of serendipity. And sometimes He smacks us in the side of the head. You'll know if you take the time to actually hear Him. Feel Him.

Try it. Ask the Holy Spirit to show you how to listen. When you slow down long enough, you'll see and feel all that you have been missing.

Here is the prayer I wrote for my stepfather:

Jan 14, 2014

Heavenly father, I come to you today to ask you to come into my heart. I surrender myself to you.

All of my life, I've depended on my own strength, mind and body instead of relying on You. Open my eyes so that I can see You in every moment. I'm no longer going to pretend that I'm stronger than I really am. Instead, I am going to lean hard on You. I ask the Holy Spirit to control my mind and soothe me from the inside out.

Lord, my situation is too heavy for me and I cannot do this alone. I ask that you carry me through them. I release it into your care and keeping. I come to you weary and burdened and you promise to give me rest. I trust You and I give you my heart.

Have mercy on me, God and forgive me of my sins. Search me Lord and know my heart. Lead me along the path of everlasting life.

If I have Any anger, bitterness or unforgiveness, Lord, I release it to you. I give all of my burdens to you.

I believe in you, Jesus and I surrender myself to you. I believe that you died for my sins and that you are the light and the way.

Touch every part of my body and soul. Fill me with your love. It is by your grace I am saved.

Amen

Chapter 9: Why?

Sometimes we find ourselves in situations we don't particularly like. We wonder why this door won't open so we can move onto something else. We question why we can't seem to close the door on something we DON'T want to go through. We get anxious because we have no control over what happens and what it all means.

Why is this all happening, God? We debate in our minds.

WHY? Why do I have to suffer through this?

That's our worldly view. We can only see what is in front of us. The view from our level.

It is a difficult realization that when you look at things solely from your limited view, stuff is just going to make NO sense (to you). As soon as you accept this reality, trust comes in. That's hard. I know.

I am going through something right now, and I have asked God these same questions: "What's the purpose, God? Why can't I be my old self again? What if I can never hike again or exercise the way that I once did? Why would You take that away from me, God?"

It is super easy to get angry, edgy, and stressed out. Sad even. But I have to stop myself from going down that thought path. So do you if you have something like this going on in your life and are asking the same questions.

God reminds me lately in every single text I read—in any religious book, any piece of philosophical literature--that the key to living the life He wants me to live (wants YOU to live) is to live in complete dependence on Him. And with that comes absolute trust and living in the PRESENT moment.

He literally has been telling me this every day, "Basically, stop worrying about stuff, Jen. Everything is going to be OKAY. I promise. There is a reason, you just can't see it because you are looking at it too closely. You should see what I am seeing! It is spectacular."

My mind wanders back to the time of Adam and Eve (before the apple catastrophe) and how they initially lived the way that God intended for them to live. Present moment. Complete dependence. Perfect trust.

They didn't worry about a darn thing. No ego was involved whatsoever. They were fulfilled and had no reservations about the past, present, or future. Their lives were very present and perfect with no shame or distractions. THAT is how were intended to live. They had God right there with them. Can you even imagine what that must have been like?

Until they screwed it up and ate that apple. Stopped trusting. Introduced shame. Initiated the ego. Ushered in worry. Presented sin. Got acquainted with pain. Nothing has been the same ever since.

Why?

Until you recognize that in order to live the life that God has intended for you--for all of us--you have to be "old school." Not like 1990's old school, I am talking reallllyyyyyyy old school. "In the beginning" old school.

Complete dependence and complete trust. Realization that what WE see is not what God sees, and His ways are infinitely better than ours--even when we don't see it. You should see what I'm seeing! God whispers to us in our daydreams and prayers.

He wants to show us awareness that we are not meant to just "get through" life – we're meant to enjoy it. So, stop worrying about stuff that 1) we have no control over and 2) may or may not happen. How much time and energy do we waste trying to fit our life into a box that it is not meant to fit into?

Ask yourself, "What kind of life do I want to live?" The one filled with love, tender moments, gratitude in my heart, laughter, freedom from doubt, and laughter? Or the one filled with worry, questions, anxiety, and sadness?

Amidst the crappiest of days, when we look up, we can see God's miracles everywhere. It has been through my suffering that I have realized just how much I actually NEED Jesus to get me through it.

Sure, I can sit here and keep asking, "Why?" But what good would that do? Exactly.

I want to be totally open to the possibilities of the day--

each day--to be vulnerable to the lessons that day is trying to teach. I want to have a smile on my face instead of a scowl. I want to trust instead of question. I want to accept "what is" and use it as a lesson to learn and grow.

I want to be a light and to leave a mark in this world instead of a dark spot. I want to trust You every day, God.

I know You got this, and there's a reason for it. Your grace is sufficient.

Thank You, God.

> The Lord is my light and my salvation—whom shall I fear? The Lord is the stronghold of my life—of whom shall I be afraid?
>
> **— PSALM 27:1, NIV**

> Now the man and his wife were both naked, but they felt no shame.
>
> **— GENESIS 2:25, NLT**

> What he opens, no one can close;
> and what he closes, no one can open:
>
> "I know all the things you do, and I have opened a door for you that no one can close."
>
> **— REVELATIONS 3:7-8, NLT**

Chapter 10: Chaos

Stop worrying. Hear His voice. Quiet your mind. Relax. Think His thoughts. Don't let your mind wander. Be present. Don't conform to the patterns of this world. Seek His face. Trust Him with ALL of your thoughts. Be thankful regardless of the circumstances. That is a lot of stuff to think about.

When you feel the clatter of the chaos in the world we live in, it's so easy to be agitated, worried, and anxiety-ridden.

Meanwhile, God is sitting there much like a child who yearns to be called on in class, putting His hands up, moving feverishly in His seat saying, "Ooh, ooh... look at ME. Look at ME. Call on Me! I know all of the answers! You can find joy and peace in me!" He tries in so many ways to get your attention. Do you call on Him? Or do you ignore Him?

Deuteronomy 36: 1 (NIV) says, "Be strong and courageous. Do not fear or be in dread of them, for it is the Lord your God who goes with you. He will NOT leave you or forsake you." This passage shows that the simple act of acknowledging this during each day gives you strength, courage, and comfort.

Are you constantly afraid and anxious because the news is on twenty-four-seven, and all you do is sit on the couch with the turmoil of the world in the background and social media agitating you on your phone? If so, you can't possibly find the peace that is right in front of your face... staring right at you. God is sitting there, waving His hands, saying, "Search for me. Look at me! Pick me, Pick me!"

You must quiet your mind so that you can recognize the holy hungers that your soul so desperately desires. FOCUS ON THESE things:

Stillness.

Gratitude.

The beautiful sunset in front of you.

The loved one(s) in your home.

The good food.

The great glass of wine.

An exciting conversation.

A prayer.

A loving relationship.

Your life.

Your blessings.

Your health.

The very breath you take.

The shining sun.

The light of the moon.

The beauty of nature.

The present moment.

Now those, my dear friends, THOSE are the moments that are so meaningful amidst the mayhem that surrounds you in this broken world.

It is NEVER too late (unless you are dead, then I am afraid it is) to start a relationship with God. One of my favorite quotes is this: I have given God a million reasons not to love me, and NONE of them changed His mind. I have done probably over a million crappy things in my life, and I can assure you that Christ loves me anyway.

He will change you from the inside-out. The changes will be subtle at first, then one day you will wake up, and the shell of the person you once were will be gone, and the new you will brilliantly emerge. You won't even recognize yourself. You will look back and wonder how you could have lived all of those years without Him and His presence.

You will find that the things that once scared you and made you anxious are no more. After all, you have love with you and within you.

Instead of curling up in a ball on the floor because you can't breathe when life's circumstances punch you right in your stomach, you will pause, be still, and be grateful. You will confidently stand right back up because you will realize that you are right where you are supposed to be. There is a reason for all of it.

You will dust yourself off and politely tell the devil, "Thanks for the advice, but I am not listening." You will realize that any struggle is part of "your plan" even when, in your head, it really wasn't part of your plan. It's His plan for you, and you will be okay with it even when it makes no sense (to you).

You will also realize that if you only relied on your strength, you would be in trouble. Things would be much different. Not in a good way.

So today, I urge you to go confidently about your day. When the discord of the world taps you incessantly on the shoulder beckoning you to run and hide and to be afraid, turn around. Look at him and proclaim *that you are NOT afraid because God is with you. Amen.*

> Do not conform to the pattern of this world, but be transformed by the renewing of your mind. Then you will be able to test and approve what God's will is—his good, pleasing and perfect will.
>
> **— ROMANS 12:2, NIV**

> He is the Rock, his works are perfect, and all his ways are just. A faithful God who does no wrong, upright and just is he.
>
> **— DEUTERONOMY 32:4, NIV**

Chapter 11: Solitude

It is in solitude that you will realize that you are really never alone. We have this soul within us that shines bright and is different and unique... so very distinct from all others. We have a destiny to fulfill that is beautiful, good, and eternal.

We should learn to look at ourselves with the same delight, joy, and satisfaction with which God sees us in every moment. That would be amazing, wouldn't it? Imagine how great the world would be if we all did this.

We totally can because He is within us. So, we are never alone, you see. Nothing, including the brightest days to the darkest days, can separate us from His love.

Wouldn't it be great if we all looked at ourselves with such love and went through each day looking for our blessings in each moment? If we responded to everything that happens to us with gratitude and acceptance? The dark times wouldn't seem so dark. We would realize they are temporary and that there is good happening, even when we can't readily see it.

The light times would be so much brighter.

My prayer for you today is one of my favorites. It is called, "The Deer's Cry."[1]

I arise today

The Storm

Through God's strength to direct me,

God's might to hold me,

God's wisdom to guide me,

God's eye to look before,

God's ear to hear me,

God's word to speak to me,

God's hand to guard me,

God's way to lie before me,

God's shield to protect me,

God's host to save me from snares of devils

From temptation of vices,

From everyone who shall wish me ill,

Afar and anear,

Alone and in multitude.

Chapter 12: Thou Salt Not Worry

People ask me if I am worried. They may be asking you the same thing.

Are you?

Worry sucks. It doesn't change anything. Worry is a worthless waste, and it is worldly. Worry is whacked out and weakens our weary wits. It withdraws us--makes us woeful and wonky. It is wretched and wimpy. It's the worst, and it's wrong.

WOW. How is that for alliteration? I'm laughing about how all of that came together. Nonetheless, it is all true. Worry is totally dumb.

God doesn't want us to worry! He wants us to trust Him. Worry is fear. You know how many times it says "Fear not" in the Bible? 365. One for each and every day. What do you think that God wants to pound in our hard little heads? *Everything will be OK. I have a plan. I promise. Stop freakin' worrying.*

Worry erodes our minds and lives and literally accomplishes nothing. Not ONE SINGLE THING. We cannot control the past, and we cannot control the future. God will provide. He promises that to all of us.

The Storm

The only thing we can do is trust Him. He tells us over and over that we are His children, and we have nothing to fear. He is with us, for us. When we waste our time worrying, we ruin the present moment that we are in.

We just have to take one day at a time. We will have our good days, and we will have our bad days. We have to enjoy each moment as it comes. We need to ask Jesus to be our shepherd every morning, and He will. He's good like that.

When the diagnosis comes, when the pain comes, when the suffering, the hurt and disappointment come, we cannot let those things rule us or make us into their image. We have to live our lives with purpose--on purpose.

We also need to ask God to heal us, and if that is His plan, we know He will. BUT we can't worry about it. Everything is going to be okay.

What we do know is that we should be so grateful for the time we have been given. We should be thankful for the people that surround us. We need to be appreciative for the overwhelming peace that we have found through our relationship with God.

> So do not fear, for I am with you; do not be dismayed, for I am your God. I will strengthen you and help you; I will uphold you with my righteous right hand.
>
> — ISAIAH 41:10, NIV

Thou Shalt Not Worry

Therefore do not worry about tomorrow, for to-morrow will worry about itself. Each day has enough trouble of its own.

—MATTHEW 6:34, NIV

Anxiety weighs down the heart, but a kind word cheers it up.

— PROVERBS 12:25, NIV

Consider how the wild flowers grow. They do not labor or spin. Yet I tell you, not even Solomon in all his splendor was dressed like one of these.

— LUKE 12:27, NIV

Chapter 13: Love Ripples

Most of us are not mindful of how our actions, words, and thoughts go out into the world far beyond ourselves. More than you can ever imagine, you impact more than just your immediate "circle" around you.

Imagine this: you're driving down the road, and some jerk cuts you off. Even worse, he doesn't say he's sorry or even give you "the wave" that silently says, "I messed up, I am sorry!" You immediately feel wronged, mad, upset, and angry. You find your mood changes for the worst. Maybe you carry that anger with you to the store that you were going to. Instead of being nice and kind to the cashier, you're rude and short... still steaming from the audacity that guy had cutting you off. *How dare he drive like a jerk like that? Who does he think he is?* Ripple...

The cashier that you were just short and rude to was having a sad day already. Her husband had just told her that he wanted a divorce. Now she has to deal with some rude person buying groceries. Ripple...

That's the last straw for her. She snaps at the next client that comes through her line. He is outraged. He goes home, and on the way, road rages when someone tries to get into his line in front of him. His actions, in turn, make another person mad who takes his anger out on others. The ripples you started keep spreading.

You started something that you don't even know is in motion. Hundreds of ripples get started, and they continue to spread all over the place, plus it stays with you.

When you get home, you tell EVERYONE in your house about the guy who cut you off this morning. Your voice is elevated. Your emotions are high, and your face scowls when you tell the story, "Can you believe that guy? How could he do that to me?" You're so agitated because this happened or that happened. Blah, blah, blah.

Good for you, you let someone basically ruin your day, and now you are taking part in making everyone else's day miserable. Your home, which was just filled with peace a few short minutes ago, is filled with agitation. Happy now?

So, here's the deal: Maybe next time something like that happens, instead of thinking about yourself and how mad someone like that made YOU, change your mindset. React with love. What if, instead, when the guy cuts you off, you respond with the thought, *I hope that guy is okay. I hope that he doesn't have some sort of emergency that he has to get to quickly.*

You stop the negative ripple and the hostile chain of events that could have happened. They could have been never-ending. You don't know.

The truth is, we don't know what is going on in someone

else's life. Everyone has their struggles. We don't know the suffering or the bad news someone might have heard that day. We don't know the sorrow in the minds of others or the hurt that they might be feeling.

When we choose to assume the best in people, a lot of things will change for you. Repeat after me: "It is not all about me. It is not all about me."

Maybe the guy who cut you off just got a phone call from his father telling him his mother died. The reason he is driving so erratically is because he is so distraught, and he is rushing home to be there with his father.

He could also just be a jerk.

You don't know. The question is not whether he is a jerk. The question is, which response will bring YOU more peace? Yeah, I thought so.

In whatever storm you are going through, you can still consciously choose what kind of person you want to be and how you react. You can stop the negative ripples with love ripples because those are way more powerful. Imagine if we flooded THOSE ripples into the world.

Make some new ripples. Spread gratitude, love, kindness, laughter, positivity, random acts of kindness, a listening ear, an understanding heart, peace, and inspirational thoughts wherever you go.

No one will be perfect at this. Just be mindful of everything that you put out there, and you will develop a greater sensitivity towards it. When you are putting a bad ripple out there, you will quickly recognize it and put a stop to it. Instead, turn around and put a GOOD ripple out into the world.

Your reactions are powerful, my dear friends. Their energy they have has the capability to change the world. One action, thought, and reaction at a time.

Do everything in love.

— 1 CORINTHIANS 16:14, NIV

Be completely humble and gentle; be patient, bearing with one another in love.

— EPHESIANS 4:2, NIV

Chapter 14: Trust Path

There are two ways to live our lives: OUR way or HIS way. Difficult or easy. It is your choice.

Let me explain.

The first way is YOUR way. You just go about your life not trusting in the greater wisdom and purpose of God. You wander along your path, meandering here and there. Alone. You might reach the end of the path, but along the way you become anxious and bitter. You don't see the beauty on the trail because you're so focused on how bad the path sucks. It's in the full sun, hard and steep.

It's all about you and your abilities--you don't need anyone. You think that whatever happens is just random with no meaning, and you hate the world for it because you are suffering. Yeah, you can still get over things, but life is just, well, whatever.

OR

You can walk along the "Trust Path." This trail is direct. It's beautiful. Shaded. God is right there with you, walking the path. You stay right on it because you trust that He is leading you right where you are supposed to go. Sure, things happen along that way that might suck, but you know they're temporary and that there is a purpose for them, so it is OKAY.

The Storm

I have been on both paths before, and there is no spoiler alert as to which one is better...

> Trust in the Lord with all your heart and lean not unto your own understanding, in all your ways acknowledge him, and he will make your paths straight.
>
> — **PROVERBS 3:5-6, NIV**

> He replied, "Because you have so little faith. Truly I tell you, if you have faith as small as a mustard seed, you can say to this mountain, 'Move from here to there,' and it will move. Nothing will be impossible for you."
>
> — **MATTHEW 16:20, NIV**

> Wait for the Lord; be strong and take heart and wait for the Lord.
>
> — **PSALM 27:14, NIV**

Chapter 15: Are You a Martha or a Mary?

There is a passage in the Bible (Luke 10:39-42) about two sisters--Martha and Mary. To paraphrase, the story goes a little something like this:

Jesus comes into a town called Bethany. He goes to Martha's house, and she basically spazzes out like most of us do when someone important is coming over. She is so concerned about impressing Jesus that she is feverishly cooking, cleaning, preparing in order to make her home ready for her important guest. Jesus is at her house, and Martha is too busy doing all of those things that "have" to be done (in her mind, so that she could perhaps impress Jesus) while THE MOST IMPORTANT action that should have been done is completely ignored: spending time with and giving her attention to Jesus.

Her sister, Mary, gets it. She doesn't care about the preparations. She doesn't give a darn what anyone else thinks. She has Jesus in front of her, and she gives Him her full attention.

Martha gets aggravated with her sister for not helping her prepare the house and makes a snarky remark to Jesus about her. He shuts her down and basically tells her that she is unnecessarily worried and upset about things that really just don't matter. Mary had figured out what was actually important, and it was spending time with Him... listening to His words... His teachings.

Martha was soooo worried, anxious, and distracted that she missed the opportunity to show true hospitality to her guest--and that was to spend undistracted time with Him.

Then the story just ends, and we don't get to know if Martha "figured it out" or not. I hope that she did! That got me thinking this morning... am I a Martha or a Mary? Who are you?

We live in a world where it seems like EVERYTHING whirls around us at a thousand miles per hour. We are distracted when we should be still. We are anxious when we should not worry. We feel like we have to work eighty hours a week so that we can provide everything for our children. In reality though, our families and children just want to spend time with us.

We all need to learn from Mary. We need to pause long enough to discover that even though we have the most honorable intentions with our busyness, true meaning comes to us when we slow down. Spend time with God. Sit at the feet of Jesus and listen to His words. Don't worry about all that other crap.

Take time to communicate with God during your day. He will show you when you are being too much of a Martha.

Are You a Mary or a Martha?

Her sister, Mary, sat at the Lord's feet, listening to what He taught. But Martha was distracted by the big dinner she was preparing. She came to Jesus and said, "Lord, doesn't it seem unfair to you that my sister just sits here while I do all the work? Tell her to come and help me." But the Lord said to her, "My dear Martha, you are worried and upset over all these details!

— LUKE 10:39-41, NLT

Don't forget to show hospitality to strangers, for some who have done this have entertained angels without realizing it!

— HEBREWS 13:2, NLT

Chapter 16: Love and Action

I used to brag about being the best multitasker in the universe (so I thought). In my line of work--like many others--problems, phone calls, email, text messages, and constant interruptions come at me a thousand miles per hour, and they don't stop all day long. Reality.

I don't value the ability to multitask anymore. I have learned that multitasking is actually not a good thing. Being present is.

Now, don't get me wrong here. What I am about to talk about isn't easy to put into practice. It is a daily struggle of mine. However, when I do put it into play, things change for the better. I am able to accomplish more, help more people, and feel more fulfilled in my work. By being present.

What does that mean? Simply, being completely present in a moment or concentrating on one thing at a time. Giving my full attention while really listening, thinking, and understanding. This helps me be a better servant. I actually get more done by concentrating on one thing at a time.

When I serve better, I feel more accomplished. When I feel more accomplished, I want to serve more. When I practice compassion at work with my clients, they know it and appreciate it.

I call this "Love and Action."

When you're able to be present in your activities, people will take notice. I promise. They will feel that you truly have compassion for them and want to help. They feel *heard*.

So, when you are on the phone with someone, give them your full attention. Don't be typing at your keyboard or thinking of the 1,000 other things you need to do. Be present. When someone is in front of you, give them your full attention. Listen. Show them love and understanding. Be present. When you are working on a project of any sort, finish one thing at a time before you move onto the next.

I know, my dear friends, this is not an easy task. You can do it, though. Start with baby steps. Do at least one helpful thing for someone every day, and you will see what happens.

My son, pay attention to my wisdom; listen carefully to my wise counsel.

— **PROVERBS 5:1, NLT**

Listen to me; listen, and pay close attention.

— **ISAIAH 28:23, NLT**

Chapter 17:
Redefining Success.
Life in First Gear.

I used to define success as climbing to the top of my profession, being the best at what I do, and making a lot of money. It was about setting ridiculous goals and then working way too many hours trying to accomplish them. Success was about the recognition and the accolades, the build-up and the ego.

And I became all of those things. Crushed all of those goals. Got the magazine covers. Received the awards. Then, I wondered, "What's next?"

I did everything that I had set out to do, yet my soul was never satisfied. So, I set higher goals. Did MORE! There was never enough. I was at the top of my mountain with nowhere else to go...

Until I was "forced" to live my life for a while in first gear, and that gear sure has come in handy as I have traversed down the mountain.

First gear provides the lowest output of speed and the GREATEST mechanical advantage. Everyone needs to go down to first gear at some point in their lives, even if it is for a few hours or a few days a week to start.

The Storm

I know that most people (including myself, until recently) probably think of slowing down as a negative thing. We are used to going a hundred miles per hour every day. We operate in sixth gear, darn it!

We don't understand why someone would choose to work less, not take that promotion, the job, the challenge, not get that

one

last

thing

done.

But let me tell you what putting yourself in first gear does: it will lower your stress. You become okay with pretty much anything that happens and embrace it. It is still weird to me sometimes. I am like, "Who is this person in my head??"

You will take delight in the simplest things. Cooking dinner, petting the dogs, writing, journaling, doing things around the house, spending time with those that you love. Amazing things will be revealed to you.

The most uncomplicated things will bring you much joy. Your gratitude level will go up. You will feel more. Smile more. Appreciate more. Understand more.

Thinking back, I ask myself: were all those hours that I worked worth it?

NO.

Did my definition of success keep me from what was truly important in life?

YES.

Would I have changed anything in the past?

NO.

Why? Because without being in sixth gear all of the time, I would not know the joy of first gear.

If you can learn anything from me, it is this: downshifting is good sometimes. Take time to put yourself into first gear. Relax and enjoy the journey. Your body and your mind desperately need it. When you are there, REALLY be there, and stay there long enough to quiet your mind.

Most likely, you'll find that the life you have been living really wasn't the best life that you could have. Slowing down, balancing your life more, not being so stressed out all of the time... THOSE things are far more valuable than you might think. Far more precious than crushing your next sales goal.

To be real--sure, it's awesome to be rewarded and recognized for success. But just realize that at the end your life, that is not what truly matters. My gravestone surely won't say, "Here lies Jennifer. She was the top loan officer, and she was in a bunch of magazines, and she won a ton of awards." I want to make an impact. I want to help inspire others. I want to be a great wife, stepmother, sister, daughter, etc. I want to live the life that God has planned for me, not the one that I made up in my head of who I was to be.

Is God talking to you in this way? Do these words that you are reading now resonate with you? Maybe you have had them tugging you already. It is time to make a change. Downshift. Slow down long enough to be able to listen. Once you can do that, talk to God. I mean REALLY pour your heart out. Ask the Holy Spirit what He wants you to do, who He wants you to be. Take an inventory of your relationships and how you have spent your time up until now.

What does success mean to you?

Have you given the important people in your life your most important resource? (Hint: The answer is *time*.)

What changes can you make in your life to balance it better?

Then do it.

> Take my yoke upon you and learn from me, for I am gentle and humble in heart, and you will find rest for your souls. For my yoke is easy and my burden is light.
>
> — MATTHEW 11:29-30, NIV

Redefining Success. Life in First Gear.

Whoever dwells in the shelter of the Most High will rest in the shadow of the Almighty. I will say of the Lord, "He is my refuge and my fortress, my God, in whom I trust."

— **PSALM 91:1-2, NIV**

Chapter 18:
Your Challenge

Now that you have finished reading my stories about *Being Still, This Is What Matters*, I hope you've thought about times in your life where stillness and opening your heart to God's prompts have changed the direction of your life.

Take some time to journal about some of the times that God has talked to you.

Did you listen or did you ignore Him? How do you know that He is talking to you?

_____

_____

_____

_____

_____

_____

_____

_____

_____

The Storm

What happened? What would you do over?

_____

_____

_____

_____

_____

_____

_____

Is God talking to you right now?

_____

_____

_____

_____

_____

_____

_____

What are some things in your life that weren't important
when you were younger, but once an event happened in your
life (loss of a loved one, illness, loss of a job, etc.), everything changed?

_____

_____

_____

_____

_____

_____

_____

_____

From reading my stories, is there anything different that you will start doing?

_____

_____

_____

_____

_____

_____

_____

_____

Journal your own personal story about how God has taken something horrible in your life (that you thought was horrible at the time) and turned it around for good.

_____

_____

_____

_____

_____

_____

_____

_____

The Storm

_____

_____

_____

_____

_____

_____

_____

_____

_____

_____

_____

_____

_____

_____

_____

_____

_____

_____

_____

_____

_____

_____

_____

_____

_____

Your Challenge

Think about some times in your life where you worried a LOT about something that never ended up happening. What lessons can you learn from this?

_____

_____

_____

_____

_____

_____

_____

_____

_____

_____

_____

_____

_____

_____

Are you guilty of not giving people your full attention? What do you think that shows them?

_____

_____

_____

_____

_____

_____

_____

Think about some regrets that you have. What can you start doing now that will stop future regrets from happening?

_____

_____

_____

_____

_____

_____

_____

_____

Just write down whatever thoughts or prayers come into your head. Just start writing without worrying about your grammar or what order your thoughts are in.

_____

_____

_____

_____

_____

_____

_____

_____

_____

Your Challenge

_____
_____
_____
_____
_____
_____
_____
_____
_____
_____
_____
_____
_____
_____
_____
_____
_____
_____
_____
_____
_____
_____
_____
_____
_____
_____
_____
_____

PART 2:

Your Past and Your Future

Chapter 19: Your Movie

The room was dark, pitch dark as my eyes opened. So dark, in fact, that I had to blink a few times to make sure I was actually awake and truly opening and shutting my eyes. There was no noise, just stillness, which was calming and comforting even though I had absolutely no idea where I was.

A beam of light filled the room. A movie started playing from a projector from across the room. The movie was silent, and all I could hear was the flickering of the reel as it fed itself through the machine.

"Okayyyyy," I whispered, looking around to see what the heck was going on. I still didn't get it.

My eyes widened when I saw myself on the screen. It was a very different version of me, though. *What is this place?* I began to get nervous.

"Where am I?" I didn't know if I was talking to myself or to someone else in the room. So, I decided to watch myself on the screen, and it actually made me smile. Holy crap, I looked good... really good. Happy.

Within minutes, my eyes were glued to the screen as the images of me doing the most amazing things danced on the screen. I was talking, and so many people were listening and smiling. In the snapshots of the people around me, I saw by their eyes that they loved and cared for me. I saw my own smile, and it was so genuine and full of peace.

Holy cow, I wish my life was really like that, I thought.

What a plethora of accomplishments and people that I helped. There were so many! Things that I had only yearned of doing actually happened in this movie. *How did anyone know these desires?* I never actually did them.

My family and friends were in it, too. Everyone looked delighted and radiant. It was beautiful. Without even realizing it, I clasped my hands together and held them together tightly by my mouth, eagerly anticipating what was next. *This is so cool!* This movie produced such delight within me.

Now I was old and surrounded by my grandchildren at the lake house. My husband, Michael, was next to me; we were both in rocking chairs, looking at the beautiful water. We slowly rocked and held hands, and we would smile and look at each other every few minutes and mouth, "I love you" to one another. Dang, he looked so handsome still. The years had been kind to us both. We were still so much in love.

I remembered when Michael and I used to talk about sitting on our rocking chairs by the water. I wished we would have bought that land we dreamed of. We got too busy though with work and never did it.

Finally, the movie ended, and tears were running down my face. What a beautiful life I had in this movie. I was happy to have seen it but also disheartened because my real life was nothing like that. It was very different. I felt so disappointed. Sad--even a little envious of the "other Jen" that got to be in the film.

A deep voice came from within the room and gently said, "This could have been your life, you know. It was the life that I had planned for you, but you didn't listen. You, my dear child, didn't use the gifts that you were born with... You did your own thing instead of what I made you to do and who I created you to be."

I found myself weeping.

"I didn't know. I didn't know. Give me another chance. I want to live that life. The one I was supposed to," I pleaded.

God had given me a glimpse of what my life could have been, which was so very disparate from the life I had led. Sure, my current life's movie was okay... but this one... THIS one was so much better because it was the authentic version of me. Who I was meant to be.

I was filled with regret. I knew I screwed up royally. "Let me go back and do things differently. Let me go back."

When you think about the life you have led so far--I mean REALLY think--the quiet-your-mind-soul-searching kind of think--have you lived the life that God meant for you to have? The life you were created to have?

Did you use your gifts?

Did you serve others?

Did you love enough?

Try hard enough?

Listen to God enough?

Help others enough?

Learn enough?

Do enough?

Spend time in prayer and stillness?

Treasure moments?

Savor relationships?

Were you grateful?

Give praise enough?

Kind enough?

Trust God enough to realize He's got you?

Take chances enough?

Have the relationships with God and with loved ones that you ought to?

Did you live to your full potential? Or were you a robot that just shuffled through life with your head down and went through the motions every day?

The good news is if you are reading this, it is not too late. You have some time to make some changes.

You know... those changes you want to make that have been fluttering through every fiber of your being for quite some time now, but you have ignored them. Those ones that you have been too busy to pay attention to. The ones that scare you. Yeah, those.

You now have time to get your priorities straight. *Maybe--just maybe--there is a reason for this difficult time I am going through*, you think. Oh yes, definitely.

"May you have awareness of the precious gift I am giving you," God whispers to your soul. Another chance.

All you have to do is reach out your hand and grab His. He's been waiting. Let Him show you the life that He had planned for you. Pause long enough to listen and actually hear it. Feel it. He will show you the way.

Today is a better day. It is a new beginning. Imagine yourself in the future. Close your eyes and think about some alterations you need to make with this precious life you have been given. Pray about them. Surrender to His will. You have lived your way for far too long. Listen. Be still. Find peace. Thy will be done, not my will. I know you are tired and weary, but in Him, you will find rest.

Today, may you see God's many miracles that you didn't notice just yesterday. I hope you smile when you realize that they have been there the whole time. "I get it now," you say out loud. Appreciate your stillness and respite for a while. Your spirit needs it. There is a significance for this time for you, so do not waste the chance that you have been given.

You do have the ability to have the life that you would look back on from your deathbed from and smile. Job well done, my dear one. Job well done.

I leave you today with my favorite Psalm, 139 (NIV):

For the director of music. Of David. A psalm.

You have searched me, Lord,

and you know me.

You know when I sit and when I rise;

you perceive my thoughts from afar.

You discern my going out and my lying down;

you are familiar with all my ways.

Before a word is on my tongue

you, Lord, know it completely.

You hem me in behind and before,

and you lay your hand upon me.

Such knowledge is too wonderful for me,

too lofty for me to attain.

Your Movie

Where can I go from your Spirit?

    Where can I flee from your presence?

If I go up to the heavens, you are there;

    if I make my bed in the depths, you are there.

If I rise on the wings of the dawn,

    if I settle on the far side of the sea,

even there your hand will guide me,

    your right hand will hold me fast.

If I say, "Surely the darkness will hide me

    and the light become night around me,"

even the darkness will not be dark to you;

    the night will shine like the day,

    for darkness is as light to you.

For you created my inmost being;

    you knit me together in my mother's womb.

I praise you because I am fearfully and wonderfully made;

    your works are wonderful,

    I know that full well.

My frame was not hidden from you

    when I was made in the secret place,

The Storm

when I was woven together in the depths of the earth.

Your eyes saw my unformed body;

all the days ordained for me were written in your book

before one of them came to be.

How precious to me are your thoughts,[a] God!

How vast is the sum of them!

Were I to count them,

they would outnumber the grains of sand—

when I awake, I am still with you.

If only you, God, would slay the wicked!

Away from me, you who are bloodthirsty!

They speak of you with evil intent;

your adversaries misuse your name.

Do I not hate those who hate you, Lord,

and abhor those who are in rebellion against you?

I have nothing but hatred for them;

I count them my enemies.

Search me, God, and know my heart;

test me and know my anxious thoughts.

Your Movie

See if there is any offensive way in me,

and lead me in the way everlasting.

Can I get an AMEN?

Chapter 20:
Under Construction

Under construction. Yeah, that is what we will call it. We are all under construction until the day we die, right?

The question is: Who is your carpenter? Who are you going to hire to build your temple?

The first guy, boy he is cheap. He tells you so many times and stresses how easy it will be to work with him. Minimal effort. You can do whatever you want to. Things will move along just fine. He doesn't have any plans, and he's just going to wing it. He's been doing this for a while, so he knows that he's doing. He is so anxious to be hired. *Why is he so cheap?* you wonder.

He makes all of these promises to you about this beautiful temple that he will build for you in the sand, right on the beach. Oh my, now THAT sound wonderful!

"You just wait and see," he says.

After you have hired this one, you quickly realize that he shows up late every day and is unreliable. His work is garbage, you have to have him redo pretty much everything he touches over and over again, and it's never "just right." Instead of two-by-fours, he uses particleboard! Your temple is in desperate need of repair. It's crap, and you know it. You wonder if it's too late. The temple that you built on the sand just washes away when the water comes.

You took the "easy way," and now you're paying for your monumental mistake. Big time.

Fire that dude! He is no good. You don't want the cheapest carpenter--you want the best, my dear friends. This guy costs you so much more than just your time and aggravation. There are eternal consequences as well.

Then, you call the one that you didn't originally hire. He sounded too good to be true. You incorrectly thought that there was a catch to what He was saying. He called himself the Great Architect, but you didn't believe Him. Now, you regret it.

He told you about how very important it was to build your temple on solid ground. He said that He would always show up on time because He will always be on the job site to begin with. Every time you call on Him, He will be there waiting for you.

You thought that working with Him would be way more effort on your part--this surrendering, trusting, and praying stuff--but is it really?

This contractor... He keeps His promises and answers when you call.

Every single time.

Under Construction

He builds your temple with materials that never fade or collapse. They remain the same, day after day. Every single nail is placed carefully and willfully for YOU because He loves you. He sacrifices Himself every day to help you build your temple.

When the floods come, your building will stand strong because the Mighty Carpenter built it. You realize that He is actually much less expensive than the first dude--He's free. All you had to do was call on Him, and He would be there to help.

It's too late! you think. I already hired the other guy. I can't start over.

Yeah, you can.

You just have to ask. The Mighty Architect can tear down the junk that was built before Him and rebuild your temple. It doesn't matter what has already happened and what has been done. It is never too late to start over. He can renew everything. The renovation might hurt a little, but it will be worth it. Promise.

Today, I want you to ask yourself, "Which carpenter do I want to hire?"

After all, your temple will be under construction until the day you die. Who do you want working on it?

Therefore everyone who hears these words of mine and puts them into practice is like a wise man who built his house on the rock.

— MATTHEW 7:24, NIV

Under Construction

A song of ascents. Of Solomon.

Unless the Lord builds the house,

    the builders labor in vain.

Unless the Lord watches over the city,

    the guards stand watch in vain.

In vain you rise early

    and stay up late,

toiling for food to eat—

    for he grants sleep to[a] those he loves.

Children are a heritage from the Lord,

    offspring a reward from him.

Like arrows in the hands of a warrior

    are children born in one's youth.

Blessed is the man

    whose quiver is full of them.

They will not be put to shame

    when they contend with their opponents in court.

—PSALM 127, NIV

For we are God's handiwork, created in Christ Jesus to do good works, which God prepared in advance for us to do.

— EPHESIANS 2:10, NIV

Chapter 21: Today

Today, I want to pray for you. My prayer for your agitated, depressed, angry, hurting, and anxiety-ridden soul is this:

That you give God your hurt, your weakness, and your sorrow.

And that you realize that we are ALL children of God, regardless of color and background.

That the Holy Spirit helps you see past your circumstances and fills your hearts with hope.

That you are protected from Satan's lies and discouragement.

That God will heal every broken place within you, and that He showers His grace upon you.

That you ask for forgiveness for your sins and start your life anew.

That you have the wisdom to seek God first each day, before anything else.

That you forgive, let go, and realize that the only way to move forward in your life is to move forward with God, in peace and freedom.

That you pray for those who have hurt you.

That you pray for God's strength and understanding and for Him to walk closely beside you each and every day.

That God teaches you what He wants you to learn during these difficult times.

That you realize that God will use this time of suffering for some good in some way, and that everything is possible with Him.

That you take this journey that you are on and realize that change happens from the inside-out and it begins with you taking responsibility and accountability first.

That you be a light in the world.

Amen

> In the same way, let your light shine before others, that they may see your good deeds and glorify your Father in heaven.
>
> — MATTHEW 5:16, NIV

> Then Jesus told them, "You are going to have the light just a little while longer. Walk while you have the light, before darkness overtakes you. Whoever walks in the dark does not know where they are going."
>
> —JOHN 12:35, NIV

Today

I lift up my eyes to the mountains—

where does my help come from?

My help comes from the Lord,

the Maker of heaven and earth.

— PSALM 121:1, NIV

Chapter 22: Cancer Is One of the Best Things That Has Happened to Me.

That statement is 10,000% true. I would not be who I am if I did not have cancer back in 2007. I also would not be alive today if I had not had the disease back then. You will see why as you read further in this book.

Don't get me wrong, it absolutely sucked while I had cancer and the subsequent aftermath of having to go through the treatments. I mean totally sucked monkey balls. Cancer is very sad to me, as I have seen it take many people that I have known and loved. It is one of the most horrible diseases a person can have. If you survive it though, I think you owe it to the world to let your light shine. You definitely owe it to yourself.

When stuff happens to us that we don't like, we have two choices: 1) to become bitter and hateful or 2) to find the good that comes from it (albeit very difficult to find sometimes... I know).

Two Bible verses come to mind when I write this:

Philippians 4:8 (KJV) says, "Finally brethren, whatsoever things are true, whatsoever things are honest, whatsoever things are just, pure, lovely, of good report; if there be any virtue, and if there be any praise, think on these things."

Proverbs 16:9 (ESV) says, "The heart of a man plans his way, but the Lord directs his steps."

These verses show both choices. How am I going to react? I mean, I HAD my whole life planned... but it wasn't what God planned for me. I had to accept that, and I could be pissed about it and let it ruin the rest of my life, or I could fight knowing that something good would come out of my healing.

I also very strongly believe that your attitude strongly determines your "healing factor," and that if you think positively, you will indeed heal faster and stronger. The opposite is also true. What we put into the world for sure effects our outcome. I chose to change my life (it is what came after it that made everything so wonderful).

Part one, I made the first changes--I started taking care of myself. Watching what I eat (nothing from a box!), how much I eat, and quality of food became important. I stopped drinking pop (as us Buffalonians say). I ate mostly a very alkaline diet. Ninety-nine percent no junk food and no processed food unless not given a choice.

I stopped smoking. I started working out, specifically

hiking to start, which has become a huge passion of mine.

An amazing thing started to happen... I FELT and looked way better. Younger. I tell people that I feel better now in my forties then I did when I was in my twenties-thirties! It's true. For so many years, I ate what I wanted and basically didn't do anything for exercise. And I was an "old person." Lord knows what my old age would have been like if I would have kept on that path. Yuck. Oh wait, I would be dead.

Part two... I started LIVING. I mean really living. I appreciated everything. I saw the good in everything and miracles everywhere. I had joy. I stopped working crazy hours (like, I used to work every day) and started taking breaks to go on vacation. I realized that there would never be a "good time" to go on vacation in my industry, so I just started going. I found out that the world didn't end because Jennifer took a week off.

I saved money, but not too, too much, and then have spent the heck out of the rest. I have it set up where I will be comfortable when I retire, but I have also guaranteed that I can do what I want with my CURRENT time here, to have fun and do good with it! I realized that the more you give away, the more God blesses you... and then you give away more... and then God continues to bless you. What a great circle that is.

So, there you go. That is my story. I chose not to be afraid, and somehow, I just knew that everything was going to be okay. I trusted God. He helped me figure it out. He took a horrible thing and showed me how to use it for good to change my path in life... the one that He intended me to be on.

When things like a cancer diagnosis happen, it is easy to lose sight of what is really important. This life is temporary. Heaven is eternal. We don't have all of the answers. We have to trust. We HAVE to trust. WE HAVE TO TRUST.

Anything that happens--EVERYTHING that happens-- will have good come out of it if we take the time to pause and trust our Mighty Savior. This path isn't so easy at first. We look for answers. We like knowing what is going to happen. We like closure and concrete explanations and solutions. I get it. He gets it too.

But wanting answers doesn't mean we are going to im- mediately know what the good is. That is where the trust comes in. We have to praise God when things are good and when they aren't so good too. When we win and when we lose, thank the Lord.

When we choose to look for and find the good in a situ- ation, no matter how bad it is, you'll find a peace that can't be taken from you.

But blessed is the one who trusts in the Lord,

whose confidence is in him.

They will be like a tree planted by the water

that sends out its roots by the stream.

It does not fear when heat comes;

its leaves are always green.

It has no worries in a year of drought

and never fails to bear fruit.

— **JEREMIAH 17:7-8, NIV**

Commit your way to the Lord;

trust in him and he will do this:

He will make your righteous reward shine like the dawn,

your vindication like the noonday sun.

— **PSALM 37:5-6, NIV**

Chapter 23: I Had a Plan. It Did Not Work Out. I Bet You Did Too.

I originally wrote this about a year ago.

I used to have this plan as to how my life would be. I would be married, have one-to-two kids, be a successful doctor, and we would live somewhere cool like Colorado or Sedona or something.

Then, life happened.

Marriage has not worked out for me so far, although one day I would like to try again. Obviously, since I never even finished college, I am not a doctor. I live in San Antonio. I have no kids. I don't have a white picket fence--I have a black metal one.

I TRIED to have kids. I practiced and practiced (LOL) and practiced--and have never gotten pregnant. I don't know if it was the fact that I only have one stupid ovary (because I had a tumor when I was fifteen, and they took my other one out) or all of the surgeries I have had since then for cysts or the radioactive junk I had to put into my body for my cancer treatments. Whatever! All I know is that it just isn't in God's plan for me.

The Storm

I have also tried two rounds of in-vitro. That was such a distress on my body and pocketbook. I did two rounds of this. On the second round, I actually had two eggs fertilized, and they survived for four days. For those of you who don't know, the embryo has to survive for five days to be implanted. I was SO excited. I was willing to take the risk of being pregnant.

For me, pregnancy is VERY high risk due to the lovely blood clotting disorder that I was born with. There was a definite risk of death for me, but I was willing to take it. Day five came, and I was at the doctor's office preparing for my implantation... only to find out that they had literally just died. Heartbreak.

It just wasn't in His plans. I am okay with that--now. I wasn't back then. I was pissed. I would see all of these girls all around me make love one time and get pregnant with kids they really didn't want, and it honestly used to really make me mad.

You are probably wondering why I just didn't adopt a child. Thinking back, I wish I would have years ago, but I wanted to try and have my own. Then as the years have passed, I just didn't want to raise a kiddo by myself. I wonder now that I am in my forties what God has in store for me. Part of me figures that I will end up with a dude that has kids, but they won't ever be MY kids.

So, what to do...

I Had a Plan. It Did Not Work Out. I Bet You Did Too.

It is hard for me to even hold a baby sometimes because I could never have one. Is that weird? Maybe. I am not sure if it is subtle jealousy or that the action just causes me so much pain and sadness.

What DOES make me sad is that I cannot make my parents grandparents. Cause they would be great grandparents. I see their eyes when they see their brother's and sister's kids have kids of their own. I know that it makes them envious and sad. I know that they yearn to be grandparents, and that is a present that I have not given to them.

I have such a close relationship with my parents that part of me cannot imagine not having a child of my own, and the other part of me wonders if I have become too selfish with my time to have one of my own. I would be a darn good mom though.

It scares the heck out of me when I think that I will not ever have one of my own, and then it also scares the heck out of me to raise one ON my own. I know that I would and could provide an amazing life for a child. I know I can.

As I write this, man, it has been some great freakin' therapy for me! LOL.

My "gut" (which is God to me) tells me that I will be a mom one day, when it is right.

So, what is my point for today? We make plans, and God laughs sometimes. He knows best and will give us what is needed at the right time. Sometimes the things we dream of really aren't what is the best for us. We just need to sit back and relax. He's got this.

Fast forward to a year later.

I am now married and have two wonderful stepchildren. For the first time in my dating life (and I am being real here), I actually love them and love being a stepmom. You see, THIS is what God had planned for me. It has worked out perfectly.

It will for you, too. We just have to be patient. We cannot force things. They will come at the right time. You will see. We can make all of the plans we want to, but if it is just not right, they won't happen. So, when things don't work out the way you want them to, trust God enough to know that everything will be okay.

I Had a Plan. It Did Not Work Out. I Bet You Did Too.

"For I know the plans I have for you," declares the Lord, "plans to prosper you and not to harm you, plans to give you hope and a future. Then you will call on me and come and pray to me, and I will listen to you. You will seek me and find me when you seek me with all your heart.

— JEREMIAH 29:11-13, NIV

Many are the plans in a person's heart,

but it is the Lord's purpose that prevails.

— PROVERBS 19:21, NIV

Chapter 23: Playing It Safe

There's a parable in the Bible that came to my mind this morning. I'm sure that most of you have heard about it and perhaps read it a time or two.

It is in Matthew 24, and it reads:

> The Parable of the Bags of Gold
>
> "Again, it will be like a man going on a journey, who called his servants and entrusted his wealth to them. To one he gave five bags of gold, to another two bags, and to another one bag each according to his ability. Then he went on his journey. The man who had received five bags of gold went at once and put his money to work and gained five bags more. So also, the one with two bags of gold gained two more. But the man who had received one bag went off, dug a hole in the ground and hid his master's money.
>
> "After a long time the master of those servants returned and settled accounts with them. The man who had received five bags of gold brought the other five. 'Master,' he said, 'you entrusted me with five bags of gold. See, I have gained five more.'
>
> "His master replied, 'Well done, good and faithful

servant! You have been faithful with a few things; I will put you in charge of many things. Come and share your master's happiness!'

The man with two bags of gold also came. 'Master,' he said, 'you entrusted me with two bags of gold; see, I have gained two more.'

"His master replied, 'Well done, good and faithful servant! You have been faithful with a few things; I will put you in charge of many things. Come and share your master's happiness!'

"Then the man who had received one bag of gold came. 'Master,' he said, 'I knew that you are a hard man, harvesting where you have not sown and gathering where you have not scattered seed. So I was afraid and went out and hid your gold in the ground. See, here is what belongs to you.'

His master replied, 'You wicked, lazy servant! So you knew that I harvest where I have not sown and gather where I have not scattered seed? Well then, you should have put my money on deposit with the bankers, so that when I returned I would have received it back with interest.

"'So take the bag of gold from him and give it to the one who has ten bags. For whoever has will be given more, and they will have an abundance. Whoever does not have, even what they have will be taken from them. And throw that worthless servant outside, into the darkness, where there will be weeping and gnashing of teeth.'"

— MATTHEW 25: 14-29, NKJV

The third dude totally played it safe. He had been given an ability, and he did nothing with it. He was too scared to take the chance. He buried it until its potential shriveled up and died.

Another way to interpret that story is this: there are those who have the ability to DO, yet they do nothing because they're scared to take the chance. Then there are those that DO. The risk-takers. Those who are not afraid to use their God-given "talents" the way that He intended them to be used. They know that they have been given a chance to make a difference, to teach, to inspire, to learn, to lead--they actually use their gifts to make it happen. They live the life that they were intended and designed to.

Those who are brave enough use their abilities and are given many chances to do so. God likes when we use our talents. The more we use them, the more we will have further opportunities to let them shine.

The opposite is also true.

We pray for change, and when given the privilege to participate, we squander the chance because it is easier to "play it safe" and just bury things because we are lazy or scared. Then we wonder and begin to live a life of "what-ifs."

What IF I would have taken that chance? What IF I would have written that book? Talked to that person? Opened my heart to that change? What IF I used my ability to sing... write... play?

Today you have a choice to make: do you use your gifts, or do you stow them away? Do you live the life that God destined you to have, or do you live your live un-lived because you didn't believe in yourself?

We ALL do this. We doubt ourselves, and we certainly don't give ourselves enough credit. We don't spend time on US long enough to grow the skills we were born with. We compare ourselves to others. *Oh, I can't sing like so-and-so, so I just won't sing at all. I can't write like James Patterson, so what's the use? I can't lead like the President, so I just won't lead.* We tell ourselves these stupid things in our heads.

When we say it out loud, we realize how silly it is to compare our gifts with anyone else's. So what if you aren't like the others? You are YOU, and there is a reason for that. We aren't meant to be like anyone else.

For about a year, I have been doing this very same thing. I had the ability to write a book or a devotional. In the beginning, I didn't want to believe it myself. Now, I wholeheartedly agree that this is something that God has intended for me to do, and He has given me ample opportunity to do so.

We can all agree that I have certainly had enough of life

experiences to fill a few books. LOL. I have so many lessons to share and words in my mind that can inspire others. *Oh, but Jennifer, you are a loan officer... you aren't a writer.* I have told myself this line about a thousand times. I have been afraid to take that chance. Do SOMETHING with my talent. What if I fail? Holy crap, that would be so embarrassing. What if everyone hates it? What if it is horrible?

It is funny how God works. He makes me laugh sometimes.

Through my most recent suffering, I have had a LOT of time off work. More than I have ever had had in twenty-five years. He has given me some of the best insights and ideas that I have EVER had... and I have written them all down. He also had several people call me. It was the most random group that I could imagine. None of them knew each other. My customers, friends, and acquaintances called to tell me that God told them that I was supposed to write. I was supposed to share my stories and testimonies with others. I had a gift, *so please don't waste it.*

And so, my journey began. I took the four months that I had off work, and I wrote this for those who are going through hardship, be it from a loss of a job, an illness, loss of a loved one, feeling lost, sadness, trauma. Any life changes. My goal is that it will help you cope and thrive.

When in my life will I ever get four months off work again? Probably not until I am retired. I took what was in most people's eyes seen as a horrible hardship, and I used it for good. I believed that this was what God intended for me to do.

If I can help just ONE person, then my talents won't be wasted. I sure hope it is more than that though.

Chapter 24: 4 A.M. Conversations

In the tranquil moments before sunrise, I lie in bed, wide awake with tears running down the sides of my face into my hair. I am lying there, just looking up into a ceiling that I cannot see.

Waiting.

A million things run through my mind that kept me stirring all night, never quite letting me get a good sleep.

"Lord, take this worry from me," I pray.

Stop worrying about what you don't know yet, there is no use. Worrying does not add one hour to your precious life.

"This *waiting time*... it is freakin' torture, God. I know that there is something wrong with me... but what, Lord?"

I am waiting with you. I am here.

"Jesus, heal me. Please. Let the doctors find out what is wrong with me so that I can just deal with it... fix it. I am scared, Lord."

Do not be afraid, I am with you. I am your shield. I will grant you peace. You just need to be still. Please do not be discouraged my dear one.

"God, reveal to me what I am in for. I NEED to know.

How will my life be changed? Will I get back to normal?"

Your present sufferings are not worth comparing with the glory that will be revealed to you. Don't be anxious about anything, My child, but pray to Me with thanksgiving in your heart. Do not worry about tomorrow, for tomorrow will worry about itself. Be present, and we will take one day at a time... together.

"Okay, Father. I trust You. I will rest in You and wait."

My dear child, yes, trust Me with all of your heart, and do not lean on your own understanding. Remember, My love will never fail you. It rejoices in the truth, it always protects, always hopes, always trusts, and always perseveres. My love never fails.

I close my eyes, and I feel better. One day at a time. One day at a time.

This is hard to do. This *trust* thing. But when you do give God your burdens, your worries, and your sorrows, He takes them away. Rest. Trust. Have faith. Your Father loves you.

Chapter 25: Choices, Choices

Join me in imagining a little here.

How different would your life be if you were born to different parents? In a different place and time perhaps. Somewhere else.

Imagine that you were born in a different country. Maybe the Middle East. Your soul housed in your temporary body on this earth but with different parents. Weird to think about, right?

Do you believe in destiny? Do you believe that you were born in the time and place you were supposed to? I do. Mainly because I would not be here if I had been born, say, in the 1800s. My blood clots would have already killed me back in my 20s.

I believe that God makes no mistakes when it comes to His perfect timing. We are fearfully and wonderfully made... remember? We were each born with unique gifts, and we are here to live a life that is distinctly different than anyone else on this earth. Our souls are granted temporary housing in this body that we were born with, and what we do with it is really, entirely up to us. Really.

The Storm

There are so many possibilities. They are endless if you think about it. We have unlimited options of how we will use our gifts (or not use them), and we can choose to love, cherish, and take care of our "house" or not. Choices matter, even the little ones.

I am about to have a birthday this month, and while thinking about turning forty-four, it made me really ponder how my life choices got me to where I am today. Every single decision that I have made, since I was able to myself, has led me to right now.

And now...

and now!

The same thing goes for you.

The mistakes, the regrets, the smart moves, the chances, the bold moves, the dreams... all of the bazillion choices that I have made along the way got me here at this very moment.

God gave me my body and my initial circumstances in life, but He also gave me gifts to work with. It was up to me to make something out of them. I am a huge believer though that no matter what circumstance you were born into, the way that you choose to live your life is on you. You cannot let some crappy past dictate your future. You cannot blame your current chaotic life on anyone else but yourself. Cool thing though--you can change just by making different choices.

It's up to me to continue to use my gifts to live the best life that I can live. It is the same for you. Trust me, I did not have a childhood or an upbringing of rainbows and butter-flies, but I did make a decision to NOT let it dictate how I would live in the future. I used my God given qualities to live the life I live now. I embraced my uniqueness and crawled out of my darkness into the woman I am at this very second. Things could have gone very differently.

I believe a great way to start changing is to have new experiences, to try new things. This awakens our souls. Expanding your experiences might lead you to a whole different life just by trying something new. Experiences make us stronger. So many of us are stuck in a rut where we just give up because we think it doesn't matter what we do, we will still be XXX (insert your problem here). I am here to tell you, though, that this is not true.

Choices.

As we get older, the more our souls show. It shows in our faces. It becomes visible. Your eyes, your smile, the love, the sorrow, the hurt, the anger, the happiness, the joy... it is all there. What do you want yours to look like? It is up to you, ya know.

Did you take care of your temporary house? Did you use

your gifts wisely? Did you embrace your uniqueness? Or did you let your weakness dictate this short time on earth and waste the precious time that you were given?

Choices. Unlimited possibilities.

> Wise choices will watch over you. Understanding will keep you safe.
>
> — **PROVERBS 2:11, NLT**

> My gifts are better than gold, even the purest gold, my wages better than sterling silver!
>
> — **PROVERBS 8:19, NLT**

Chapter 26: The Life That Could Have Been

A long-time friend of my father's passed away today, and like most people, my reaction was sadness for his family, followed by the thought of all of our own mortality. The life of my parents, friends, other loved ones, and of course, myself. Death does that to us. It makes us pause for a little while.

Then, as my mind does most times, my initial thoughts lead me to others. My reflection then developed into me thinking about choices and how important they are, even when you don't think they are. Choices.

You don't realize how much one teeny tiny choice can affect your entire life. Your path. Your ENTIRE freakin' life. We make them every day and don't even give them a second thought.

Go left here instead of right. I want to eat this food. Sit here. Stand up. Sleep late. Sit on the couch all day. Go to work. Stay home. Work out or not work out. Take my medicine. Wash my hands. Have I turned you into a neurotic yet? LOL. That is a lot of pressure there.

And then there are bigger choices that we make, like where we will live, who we will marry, how we want to live... or what kind of person do we want to be? I think back to those choices in particular that I have made, and it is amazing how different my life would have been if I had "gone the other way" or if I had not taken the chance.

My aunt used to date my father's friend when she was younger. How disparate their lives would have been if they had stayed together. Two entire generations would not have been born. They would not exist.

His life, his child, his wife, and his family... none of it would have been the same. Choices.

I think of all of the people that I have met along the way because of the choices that I made. Would there have been a different version of those same people in a different city or state? Shoot, now I am thinking too much!

I just think that the whole concept is so fascinating though... that there is a life out there that we could have had if we had made different choices. Would that life have been better? I am sure it would have in some cases, but not in others.

Are there some choices that I wish that I would not have made? Heck, yeah. But the cool thing about choices is that you can just make some more that are good instead of stupid! :) Starting right NOW!

Some of the decisions we make will also have unknown consequences--the random stuff and the little stuff. It is just that way. We will find out soon enough.

Then I start to wonder how many parallel alternate universes there are with different versions of me living out alternative versions of myself with different choices that I had made with the same circumstances. Is that weird? Probably.

I think we should not minimize the importance of the things we do, the ideas we have, and the people that we meet. Opportunities in front of us. Past behind us. There is nothing that you can do about the "bad" or unhealthy decisions you made previously... BUT there is something you can do about the moments that present themselves to you now.

The neat thing is that right in front of you there is a way to completely take your life and put it on a different path. It would be awesome to see where God takes ya!

I guess, my point is this: instead of dwelling and wishing for the "life that could have been," you can enjoy the life that is right now. Understand that you have the ability to pick and choose things right now in this present moment. You can't change the past, but in most cases, you CAN choose stuff that would help make your future brighter.

(An example of a bad decision)

And when the woman saw that the tree was good for food, and that it was delightful to look at, and a tree to be desired in order to make one wise and insightful, she took some of its fruit and ate it; and she also gave some to her husband with her, and he ate.

— GENESIS 3:6, AMP

The wise are glad to be instructed, but babbling fools fall flat on their faces.

— PROVERBS 10:8, NLT

Chapter 27: To the One I Left Behind

To the One I Left Behind,

I have left you, and I am never coming back to you.

You were so selfish and cold-hearted sometimes. You didn't care too much about anyone else besides yourself. You lied and even cheated. You never gave anyone your full attention and had no problem running over anyone that got in your way.

You were cynical and jaded. Negative and bitter. You judged others a lot and made unfair assumptions about who they were.

Sure, you were nice sometimes, but it was only a "surface" nice because you never let anyone get too close to you. Vulnerability...nah...that wasn't your style. You preferred walls. Tall ones.

Your career came first, and it was more important than your family was. Your relationships suffered.

You didn't know all of the good things that God had in store for you. How could you? You didn't know Jesus back then. You didn't think that you needed to. You only knew what _you_ wanted you to know. You squelched that voice inside of you. You pushed that sucker so far down deep that it could not be heard no matter how loud it screamed. And boy, did it scream loudly for many years.

Until the day that you heard it. I mean, *really* heard it. And once it started talking, it never stopped. You didn't want it to. You desired it with all of your heart. Sought it out. It encompassed your mind.

And you began to change. It was subtle at first, but boy did it constantly progress until one day, you looked back and saw the shell of the person you once were... and smiled. You were completely transformed from the inside-out.

A new you emerged who was happier, joyful, loving, and peaceful. A light turned on that could not be dimmed.

And then......

I realized, it was all about the cross. Nothing was about me. It was about love and about others. It was about believing and seeking with all of my heart. It was about trusting Him with ALL of the intimate details in my life.

I realized that real meaning came from surrender, from taking out my heart and extending it out to the mighty Lord so that He could do whatever He wanted with it. This change... it STARTED with my heart.

God's Word changed hearts. My identity, beliefs, and behaviors may have changed for my time on earth, but they have consequences that last for eternity.

To The One I Left Behind

I have learned that I am never alone. He is always with me, even when I cannot see it. It is about taking God out of my back pocket or that box I've tried to shove Him in and re-alizing that He's too big for that. His presence is everywhere. I am not in control. It is His will be done, not mine and I am good--more than good, with that. Thank You, Jesus.

So, I said goodbye to the one I left behind. I am a new creation, a new being. An eternal being here on this earth for a period of time, but in heaven for eternity.

I don't miss the one I left behind. My sins are forgiven. I am cleansed. I am born again. I am saved. My life--the rest of it--will never be the same.

> I have been crucified with Christ and I no longer live, but Christ lives in me. The life I now live in the body, I live by faith in the Son of God, who loved me and gave himself for me.
>
> **— GALATIANS 2:20, NIV**

> And so I tell you, keep on asking, and you will receive what you ask for. Keep on seeking, and you will find. Keep on knocking, and the door will be opened to you. For everyone who asks, receives. Everyone who seeks, finds. And to everyone who knocks, the door will be opened.
>
> **— LUKE 11:9-10, NLT**

Chapter 28: Beautiful on the Outside

Picture a beautiful woman. A picture you have seen as you are scrolling on Facebook or Instagram, and you think to yourself, *Dang, this person has it all. She is happy, beautiful, and life looks so perfect.*

A true picture of perfection because that it the version that she wants you to see. Inside though, her life--and more importantly her heart--is a mess. She feels inadequate and empty.

Truth is, that's how a lot of us are, aren't we? We have this persona that we show on the outside, but on the inside... Oh my... That's a whole different story. We have our struggles. Our emptiness. Yearning for something that is missing inside of us that tugs our souls daily. Real life. Some of us struggle with this. It is a fact. We feel all alone. No one would love the "real" me. How could they?

What is cool is that there is someone who loves all of those wretched parts of you. Of me. Of everyone. Unconditionally. Those unsatisfactory parts that you try and hide though your outward appearance. That "person" is God.

Having a relationship with God can transform you from the inside out. It is so powerful that it can reengineer the inside of you to actually look like what you portray on the outside.

Talking to God about your struggles, your fears, and your emptiness will fill you with love, joy, and contentment. He will transform your weaknesses into strengths when you finally realize that He is with you always. He will turn your sadness into rejoicing. Doubt into conviction. Uncertainty into unwavering faith.

God is good like that. He sees and knows the real you, and He loves you anyway. Always. There is nothing in the world that you can do to separate yourself from His love. That is a fact.

So, stand up. Dust off that internal mess of yourself that you got going on and talk to God. Start a relationship. He's been waiting.

> I look up to the mountains— does my help come from there? My help comes from the Lord, who made heaven and earth!
>
> — PSALM 121:1-2, NLT

> Yes, Adam's one sin brings condemnation for everyone, but Christ's one act of righteousness brings a right relationship with God and new life for everyone.
>
> — ROMANS 5:18, NLT

Chapter 29: The Person Inside of You

The real you that has been patiently waiting to come out. The you that lives deep within. The one who wants the current "you" to come out and play. To live a little. To make those changes. To take that chance. To show your creative side.

I think most of us get into these routines so focused on just getting through the day that we forget about actually taking the time to do those things that call us, that we really want to do. That our souls want us to do. We live our lives on autopilot. We just don't make the time. A class that sounds interesting. A new hairstyle. A painting that we have envisioned. A project. A book. A vacation. A cause. A vision.

Oh, I will do it when...

Then, all of the sudden, thirty years have passed, and one day we wake up and realize that we forgot to live. We wake up and look in the mirror and wonder, *Who the heck this person is standing in front of me? What happened to me? My dreams and aspirations? The real me? Darn it. I want a do-over.* Too late.

My thought this morning is that we all need to get up, look at ourselves in the mirror, and ask if we have been living the truest version of ourselves. Have we been kind to our souls and bodies? Or have we ignored them all of these years. Have we lived?

If the answer is no, it is time to make some changes. It doesn't have to be anything drastic or crazy. Just start to recognize and act upon those little tugs that pop into your mind and won't go away. Those are the things you were meant to do. Don't wait until tomorrow. Do it now before another thirty years pass.

Here's to living the twenty-four-karat, actual, bonafide, and authentic version of the you that God made you to be.

> Teach me how to live, O Lord. Lead me along the right path.
>
> — **PSALM 27:11, NLT**

> God, you are my God; I earnestly search for you. My soul thirsts for you; my whole body longs for you in this parched and weary land where there is no water.
>
> — **PSALM 63:1, NLT**

Chapter 30: Comfortably Uncomfortable

There is something new in your life. Newness scares you. It is change.

In order to get through it, you're going to trust that someone will be there waiting for you on the other side--hand out--to catch you as you take the giant faith leap across a chasm that seems like a mile wide. In reality, it isn't a mile wide. It just seems that dang way though because in the valley below you can see snippets of the changes you are going to have to make to get there. Everything is so new. New experiences. Things are all so very disparate from the comfort that you are used to.

Ahhhh, being comfortable. It is nice to be in a place where everything is so familiar. You have security. Yeah, you know that the life you are living is filled with mediocrity. BUT change would take too much effort. It's too scary. So, instead of taking that leap to the upgraded 2.0 version of yourself that is sooo itching to break out and be free, you stay in your "comfort zone," unwilling to make yourself uncomfortable.

The Storm

Too much uncertainty, you think.

That 2.0 version within you begins to die. The better life. Better job. Better health. Stronger relationships. Serenity. Bliss. Their lights begin to fade as more time goes by without action.

Until the light goes out. The life you could have had fades away all because you were scared to take that leap. All because you don't want to be uncomfortable for a little while. You don't have faith.

What you did not realize is that God was waiting there on the other side for you the whole time. He would have picked you up if you had fallen. His hand was extended. He was always waiting for you to be ready to trust Him. Had you believed that, would you have made different decisions? I'm sure the answer is an astounding, "YES."

He would tell you that it is okay to be scared. Okay to be uncomfortable 'cause it's only going to be for a little while. Make that change. Take that chance. Put on your running shoes and take that giant leap over the chasm. Talk to Him. Ask for His guidance. He is waiting for you.

In order to realize the blessings in your life and become the very best version of yourself, you are going to have periods of time where you have to be comfortable with being uncomfortable. Yeah, it is going to be difficult. But know that even if you fall, you ARE going to be able to get right back up. Promise.

Being uncomfortable, it is difficult. It sucks. It is unpleasant. Think of the outcome though that comes from pushing through something that sucks for a little while in order to get something AMAZING. In order to be better, you cannot keep doing what you have always done. You won't ever grow.

You have to do things differently. Whether that be the perennial "get your life together" stuff like eating right, exercising, learning a new career, stopping drinking, or doing what you would actually love to do instead of working in your mundane job. Taking time for yourself. Say, "No." Say, "Yes." Try something completely new. Try a different way of doing things. Work on a relationship. Realize your internal thoughts need to change. Retrain yourself.

Learning to be comfortable with being uncomfortable will change your life.

Trust in the LORD with all your heart;

do not depend on your own understanding.

Seek his will in all you do,

and he will show you which path to take.

— PROVERBS 3:5-6, NLT

The Storm

He jumped up, stood on his feet, and began to walk! Then, walking, leaping, and praising God, he went into the Temple with them.

— ACTS 3:8, NLT

Chapter 31: 18 Things for the Younger Me

Dear younger me,

Older me wants to give you some advice about your life, so I urge you to listen. You see, you are about to embark on a journey that will take you places you have haven't even dreamed of yet. Older me wants to give tell you some things that will make your passage more enjoyable and understandable.

Here goes:

• You know that feeling that you get sometimes in the pit of your gut? You should totally listen to that. That is God talking to you.

• Who really cares about what anyone else thinks? It doesn't matter. Do your own *thang* and don't care about what "they" think.

• It is perfectly fine to fail. In fact, it is going to make us a better person.

• Having a good relationship with God is totally up to you. But, man-o-man, life is so much better when you are close to Him and spend time with Him every day. You should start this much earlier in life.

• Enjoy every second with your parents and your grandparents. They won't be around forever.

• Never, ever let anyone speak limitations into your life, no matter who it is.

• Laugh at yourself and don't take yourself so seriously. It is OKAY. Promise.

• Success won't come easy. It is not something you deserve or that is given to you. You have to work at it every day.

• When it comes to boys and relationships, realize how precious you are and that you should never ever settle for "good enough." It won't work for you.

• Save your dang money--like when you are in your twenties and forward. Save SOMETHING each week. When you get older, you will realize that savings will allow you to have more choices and freedom.

• You can do so, so much more than you think you can. You are definitely stronger than your mind makes you think you are. When the devil whispers in your ear, tell that chump to step back and get out of your way!

• Life is not going to go how you plan it in your head, and that is okay. It will actually be much better.

• Take time every day to look up and realize all that you have to be grateful for. When you do that, your life will change, and you will understand that you can be happy in any situation.

• Those tough times... yeah, those will pass. You will come out better in the end from them.

• When you are done working, actually be done working. Don't be "that person" who is constantly on their phone working when you are supposed to be spending time with your family. Give them your attention when you are with them.

• Give freely to others without expecting anything in return. A gift is not a gift if you give it with restrictions. When you realize this, you will see just how freeing it is.

• Never be afraid to "just be yourself." You are beautiful and special. Remember that.

• In life, make decisions and take chances. It is way better to ask for forgiveness than for permission. Be a leader.

Think of some things that you would tell your "younger self." I bet they are right along the same lines as mine. Take this opportunity to share your wisdom with someone much younger than you.

The Beatitudes

He said:

"Blessed are the poor in spirit,

for theirs is the kingdom of heaven.

Blessed are those who mourn,

for they will be comforted.

Blessed are the meek,

for they will inherit the earth.

Blessed are those who hunger and thirst for righteousness,

for they will be filled.

Things for the Younger Me

Blessed are the merciful,

    for they will be shown mercy.

Blessed are the pure in heart,

    for they will see God.

Blessed are the peacemakers,

    for they will be called children of God.

Blessed are those who are persecuted because of righteousness,

    for theirs is the kingdom of heaven.

Blessed are you when people insult you, persecute you and falsely say all kinds of evil against you because of me. Rejoice and be glad, because great is your reward in heaven, for in the same way they persecuted the prophets who were before you.

— MATTHEW 5:1-12, NIV

Chapter 32: On Unplugging

I just got back from my "happy place," aka Sedona, Arizona. It is a place that I love so very much and frequent as often as I am able. Maybe it is the vortex that draws me there, maybe it is the beautiful, red mountains, or maybe it is the dry desert air that my body and hair love so very much. Whatever it is, I freakin' love it there more than any other place I have visited.

In the industry that I have chosen to be in, bank loans, phone calls, texts, emails... they NEVER stop. It is a monster that we have all created and still continue (most of us) to live in. I could literally work twenty-four hours a day, and there was a point in time when I kind of did. I don't do that anymore. Thank God. People expect us to work days, nights, weekends. What the heck? I would not ever expect anyone to do this in any other industry... Why are we different?

Fast forward to where I am now. I don't, under normal circumstances, answer my phone after 5:00 p.m. or on the weekends unless it is a "loan emergency," which rarely happens because there are generally no such things as "loan emergencies." I mean, you knew you were buying a home before Saturday morning at 7:00 a.m., right? Just sayin'.

That is not to say that I don't work after 5:00 p.m. I generally work until about 6:00 p.m. every night. I will answer text messages at night sometimes, if it is a person I work with a lot or if someone genuinely needs help. I will be there to help. I promise.

It's just that a few years ago, I decided that I would not and could not let my phone/email/text dictate my life. I drew clear boundaries, and I have stuck with them ninety-eight percent of the time, which I think is pretty darn good. People thought that I was crazy, and that I would lose business. You know what? I probably have lost some, but I am okay with that. My production has doubled though since then.

We already know that I am crazy... so there you go! Boundaries. Who would have thought they worked in this industry? They do. My customers and clients who refer my business respect it. Time is the MOST VALUABLE commodity and one that we cannot get back. I have chosen to use mine wisely (to me, at least).

Back to Sedona...

I shut my phone off for four glorious days. I did not look at an email (my staff did this for me in my absence), text message, or even answer the phone. My voicemail was changed to alert people that I was out and would be back Tuesday. All was covered and good. I could completely relax.

Holy crap... that was nice. I hiked, drew a picture, attempted to watercolor another pic, journaled, drank wine watching sunsets, and thought a lot. I got Reiki. My mind and body feel good. I am back now with clear direction.

My drawing is part of a fervent effort to get back to my creative side. I am making it a priority. At least one day a week, I have been doing SOMETHING creative, whether that be gardening, painting, designing something. It just has to be something that I do with my hands with no phone. I have been writing up a storm on thoughts that I have about aging, success, God, family. You name it. Unplugging.

I think that most people, no matter what we do for a living, forget how much we need to go back to being a "kid" every once in a while. We need to play. We need to draw, paint, run, and have fun (I am also a poet! LOL). I guaranty these activities will bring back a smile on your face and satisfaction in your soul.

Be in nature. Turn your phone on airplane mode or do not disturb when you are playing so that you don't get distracted by your all-too-busy life. Pause. Unplug.

You think it's not possible to NOT work all of the time? Guess again. It is OKAY to draw boundaries. You will be very surprised how easy it is and how it won't negatively affect you like you THINK it will. You don't have to work ninety hours a week. You CAN have a life. You are worth it. There will be a day when the "old you" will cease to exist. A beautiful version of yourself can be reborn, even under the most unfortunate of circumstances. Use your time wisely. Ask the Holy Spirit to guide you in what you really are supposed to be doing. Maybe this is just it, for now.

Most likely, you never have quieted your mind enough to find out what He wants of you. Now is the time.

The Lord is my shepherd, I lack nothing.

He makes me lie down in green pastures,

he leads me beside quiet waters,

— PSALM 23:1-2, NIV

For prophecy never had its origin in the human will, but prophets, though human, spoke from God as they were carried along by the Holy Spirit.

—2 PETER 1:21, NIV

Chapter 33: Perfectly Imperfect

I used to have this visualization of what my life would be like when I got older. You know, stuff like what my house would look like, my husband, kids, career--pretty much everything in my life. I wanted them to all fit into a box I created. Things that would happen on my terms and when I wanted them all to happen. I had them all planned out. *Oh yeah... life will be so great when I... and then this will happen... and then this and this...*

Reality.

Nothing that I had envisioned in "my future world" actually occurred. In fact, most things went completely the opposite of what I had imagined them to be... the way I had *planned* them all out to happen.

It's interesting how we think when we are young. We believe that we can control our lives and that we can actually plan stuff out, and it will go exactly as calculated. No obstacles. This is what is gonna happen. *It is OUR will be done. Get out of my way!* Most of us may still think that way.

I bet God gets a really good chuckle out of that. We think we know better than He does.

I used to put God in my back pocket. Made Him small. When I needed Him, I would pull Him out, and then when I believed I was done with Him, I put Him back. *Thanks God, I am good now. Get back in there. I don't need you right now.* I didn't accept the actuality of the truth: He was bigger than that. Bigger than I could ever fathom. He didn't fit in my back pocket. Not even a little.

And, well, He knows better than I do. Always. Even when I don't understand, His ways are better than mine. His thoughts are higher than mine.

My life has been messy and unpredictable. Intoxicating and sensational. Astonishing and fascinating. Remarkable and extraordinary. I have had the deepest sorrow and the most joyous of joys. I have felt the worst heartbreak and the most exceptional unconditional love.

None of which I had planned.

Some things completely sucked while they happened-- for a little while. Until I woke up one day, and they sucked no more. I realized that things actually turned out for the best to create a better me. Well heck, I hadn't plan that.

"Of course you didn't," God whispered to my soul. "I taught you patience today.

I showed you love today.

I showed you how strong you are in Me.

I showed you how to overcome.

I showed you peace.

I showed you understanding and empathy.

I showed you dependence upon Me.

You need to slow down and be still with Me. This is your wake-up call.

I showed you that My way was way better than the one you thought you wanted."

Things could have been very different, you know. If I had an opposite mindset, I would hated my life. I would be bitter... discontented. I would have taken all of the really crappy things that have happened in my life and had a big ole pity party for myself--because only focusing on the negative things does that. I would be resentful of MY life because that perfect life I had wanted for myself didn't happen. I would blame God if I still had Him in my back pocket. *Let me pull Him out. This sucks, God. This really sucks. How could you let this happen?*

"When you feel like you are facing an impossible situation to overcome, in Me, you may have peace. In this world, you will have trouble. But take heart! I have overcome the world," He answers.

"Why does it seem like everyone else has such an easy life? Nothing ever happens to them." I ask God, "Why did I have this obstacle? That is not fair."

"Don't compare your journey with anyone else's. You

have no idea what struggles others have. I gave you all different gifts. This is the life I want YOU to have, not them. With man this is impossible, but with God all things are possible. So, rely on Me and everything will be okay. BETTER than you would have ever dreamed of. I promise."

So many people struggle, not because of their circumstances but because of their reactions to them. It is simple. You have to change your mindset. For our struggle is not against flesh and blood, but against the rulers, against the authorities, against the powers of this dark world, and against the spiritual forces of evil in the heavenly realms.

The enemy WANTS us to be pissed. Give up. Get mad. Be bitter and disgruntled. He doesn't like witnesses or examples of people who have characteristics of the loving Jesus, so he attacks our minds. Puts things in there to help us along with that suffering, to make it worse. He murmurs lies into our ears.

Don't fall for it. Pick up your head and gaze up. Learn to love your perfectly imperfect life. Your "plans" are not His plans... but oh, His plans... they are so much better **if you let them be.**

When something happens that you don't understand, let Him whisper to your spirit what He wants you to learn. Accept your situation and make peace with it, knowing that this day...

this moment...

this time...

this problem...

right now...

...will be okay. Seek His purpose, relax, and enjoy the ride.

> I have told you these things, so that in me you may have peace. In this world you will have trouble. But take heart! I have overcome the world.
>
> — JOHN 16:33, NIV

> Fight the good fight of the faith. Take hold of the eternal life to which you were called when you made your good confession in the presence of many witnesses.
>
> — 1 TIMOTHY 6:12, NIV

Chapter 34: You: Version 45.0

When we face tribulation, misfortune, adversity, and set-backs, our natural inclination is to want God to just take it all away. We don't want to hurt. We don't want to struggle. We don't want our lives interrupted.

Our inherent tendency is to ask, "WHY?... Why me?" That is our self-sufficient identity talking here. The ego. The one who thinks we do things on our own, and we don't need any stinkin' help--ever. That we're independent and don't need anyone. Just leave me alone!

This version of ourselves plays the victim and gets bitter when adversity happens. We get angry. The petulance that grows inside of us like a weed begins to take over, and we are never the same afterwards. With each tribulation, we become more and more aggrieved.

We ask for no help, but then get mad at God for not taking it all away so we can go back to our lives before the difficult times. We feel alone.

We forget what God has told us so many times.

He is here with us ALWAYS. Not sometimes.

He is OUR help and OUR shield. Not "a."

He holds us up with His right hand. He won't let us fall.

When we're dependent upon Him, we show Him that we trust Him. When we trust Him, we understand that no matter what, He will always be there... right beside us, comforting us. When we realize that He is always there, we don't give up. When we don't give up, we remain strong in Him because we realize that something great is going to come out of all of this.

Then things aren't so bad--are they? You gain confidence that no matter what, you will be OKAY. You will get through this and be even stronger after because God is with you on your side. You might not be the same afterwards, but a newer, better version of you will blossom from your pruning. You're a 2.0, 3.0, 4.0... I think I might be on version 21.0 for me.

Sure, God can take your troubles and setbacks away, but what good would that really do for you? He is using your struggles to make you stronger. Character development. Your faith grows wider, deeper each time. When you don't give up, you become stronger.

It is when we are knocked down that we are closest to our breakthroughs of where God wants us to be. Our greatest victory. Greatest testimony.

When you realize that having childlike dependence doesn't make you a weakling, you won't look at adversity the same way ever again. God could give you perfection, but He prefers you to have progress over perfection. He also totally gives us more than we can handle... it is called life. However, He tells us that we CAN handle it when we have a relationship with Him.

> For I am the Lord your God who takes hold of your right hand
>
> and says to you, Do not fear; I will help you.
>
> **— ISAIAH 41:13, NIV**

> I lift up my eyes to the mountains—where does my help come from?
>
> My help comes from the Lord, the Maker of heaven and earth.
>
> **— PSALM 121:1-2, NIV**

Chapter 35: Limitations. They Suck.

NEVER EVER LET SOMEONE ELSE LIMIT YOU OR YOUR DREAMS! EVER! Got it? Yeah, I was yelling, and I hope you got the point.

Often, it is the people closest to us who limit us. I don't think that is out of any malice or anything like that in most cases. Maybe they do it out of protection for us. People don't want to see those they love get hurt, so they try and "protect" us from failure. I think failure is a good thing though. It puts hair on your chest (like my dad used to say when we had to go through something difficult, ha ha).

Imagine if we listened to twenty percent of the limitations that others put upon us. Imagine if we listened to ALL of the limitations put upon us (which some people do!)? The "limiters" are not cognizant of what they are doing when they put those barriers on someone. Just refuse to listen. Ever.

Or maybe you are the "limiter." Are you?

Next time you are tempted to squelch someone else's dreams or wants, remember this: you don't know what God has planned for them. You don't know their gifts, their purposes, or their futures, so why would you ever speak a limitation over anyone?

Jesus replied, "What is impossible with man is possible with God."

— **LUKE 18:27, NIV**

If you then, though you are evil, know how to give good gifts to your children, how much more will your Father in heaven give the Holy Spirit to those who ask him!

— **LUKE 11:13, NIV**

Chapter 36: Words Matter

Many of us cannot fathom the impact that our words have in this world. Good or bad, our words make a difference. They are just words, right? No, no... they are more than that.

They are examples, they are dreams, they are encouragements, and they are strengths. They are hopes of a better day, empathy, belief, laughter, sadness, anger, wonder, or love. Confidence. Joy.

Words matter.

What we speak into our own lives also matters. How do you speak to yourself? What do you put into this world? What do you say when no one else is around? Do you believe in yourself? Oh, my goodness, that last one is important. If you don't believe in yourself, who will?

What do you say to others? Do you build up or do you tear down? Do you throw up all over people (figuratively, of course)? Or do you take it all in? Sometimes, what you don't say is just as powerful as what you do say.

I believe that the words we tell ourselves are the most important because from there, the words we say to others stem from within. Words matter. The best version of ourselves come from our own selves speaking love into our own hearts first.

If you believe in yourself, you can inspire others.

If you love yourself, you can speak love to others.

If you have joy in your life, you can bring joy to others...

You see how that works?

Words matter.

What are you telling yourself today?

Be kind and compassionate to one another, forgiving each other, just as in Christ God forgave you.

— **EPHESIANS 4:32, NIV**

But love your enemies, do good to them, and lend to them without expecting to get anything back. Then your reward will be great, and you will be children of the Most High, because he is kind to the ungrateful and wicked.

— **LUKE 6:35, NIV**

Chapter 37: Things to Think About

Your past and your future. There's a lot to think about. Figuring out what is important and what is not is one of the most integral keys to leading a balanced life.

Take some time to journal about some of these questions or to do some of the tasks I put in front of you. They are important parts of growing and learning about yourself.

When you were little, how did you envision your life to be when you grew up? Describe your marriage, occupation, home, etc. Really think back to the things you dreamed of as a child.

_____

_____

_____

_____

_____

_____

_____

_____

_____

_____

_____

_____

_____

What does your life look like now?

_____

_____

_____

_____

_____

_____

_____

_____

_____

_____

Do you ever find yourself comparing your life with others?

_____

_____

_____

Why do you think you do that?

_____

_____

Things to Think About

_____

_____

Think about some amazing things that have happened in your life that you DID NOT plan or even see coming. Write them down.

_____

_____

_____

_____

_____

_____

_____

_____

_____

_____

_____

What are some plans that you have had that didn't work out the way you wanted them to?

_____

_____

_____

_____

The Storm

_____

_____

_____

_____

_____

How do you think that God's way was actually better?

_____

_____

_____

_____

_____

_____

_____

_____

Is there something that has been tugging at your heart for you to do? That is God trying to talk to you. What is it?

_____

_____

_____

_____

_____

_____

Things to Think About

Think back on your life during the time before you had God in it. Then think about how different it is with Him present. What are the biggest differences?

_____

_____

_____

_____

_____

_____

_____

During the hardship that you are facing now, what good has come out of your journey?

_____

_____

_____

_____

_____

_____

What do you think the reason is for you to go through this hard time? What are you supposed to learn?

_____

_____

_____

_____

_____

_____

_____

_____

Write about five things that have happened in your life so far that seemed really bad at the time, but actually turned out to make you a better and stronger version of yourself.

In your life, how has your dependence on God helped you get through both your great and difficult times?

Things to Think About

_____

_____

_____

_____

_____

_____

_____

What would those times have been like if you didn't rely on God or if you didn't have God in your life?

_____

_____

_____

_____

_____

_____

_____

How is God going to use your temporary setback that you are going through right now to make you grow as a person?

_____

_____

_____

_____

_____

_____

_____

_____

What threshold are you in right now?

_____

_____

_____

_____

_____

_____

_____

Where do you think you are heading?

_____

_____

_____

_____

Is there someone that you know that you could encourage right now? Who is it and why? After you are done writing about them, stop and pray for them, and then call them and offer your love and supporting words.

Things to Think About

_____

_____

_____

_____

_____

What are some major choices that you have made that have sent ripple effects throughout the rest of your life?

_____

_____

_____

_____

_____

_____

_____

_____

_____

_____

_____

What do you think would happen if you prayed for guidance on more of your choices before you made them?

_____

_____

The Storm

_____

_____

_____

What choice can you make right now that would make
your life better?

_____

_____

_____

_____

_____

If you died today, what would your movie be like?

_____

_____

_____

_____

_____

_____

_____

_____

_____

_____

_____

_____

Things to Think About

What life did God intend for you to have? What will you change?

_____

_____

_____

_____

_____

_____

_____

_____

_____

What are your greatest gifts?

_____

_____

_____

_____

_____

_____

What makes you unique?

_____

_____

_____

_____

_____

The Storm

How can you use all of these qualities to serve God better?

_____

_____

_____

_____

_____

What is something that you can do now that would dramatically help you, but you have not done it because it is "way out of your comfort zone"? Write about that and what you think your life would be like after the uncomfortableness.

_____

_____

_____

_____

_____

_____

_____

_____

Write a letter to your much younger self. Include your top ten words of wisdom or advice based on things that you have learned.

_____

_____

_____

Things to Think About

_____

_____

_____

_____

_____

_____

_____

_____

_____

_____

_____

_____

_____

_____

_____

_____

_____

_____

_____

_____

_____

What words have you been speaking into your own life?
Are you positive or negative?

_____

The Storm

_____

_____

_____

_____

Have you ever been a "limiter"? If so, call and apologize to that person(s) and tell them something encouraging.

_____

_____

_____

_____

Let's talk about social media. Why do you think that it is so fake? What can you do to keep it real?

_____

_____

_____

_____

In what ways have you been inauthentic?

_____

_____

_____

_____

Things to Think About

Pick a day next week and shut your phone off. Write about how that felt. Would you do it again?

_____

_____

_____

_____

_____

_____

_____

List some things that have been heavy on your mind and that have been worrying you. Talk to God about them as you go to bed tonight. It will help you sleep better.

_____

_____

_____

_____

_____

_____

_____

Is there something that you have done that you don't believe that God will forgive you for? Confess it now and ask for forgiveness. He WILL give it to you.

_____

_____

_____

_____
_____
_____
_____
_____
_____
_____
_____
_____

What does God say when you quiet your mind?

_____
_____
_____
_____

Write a letter to your old self. Model it after my chapter titled, "To the One I Left Behind."

_____
_____
_____
_____
_____
_____

Things to Think About

_____

_____

_____

_____

_____

_____

_____

_____

_____

_____

_____

_____

_____

_____

PART 3:

Gratitude

Chapter 38: Grateful

In the faraway places of our minds, we have two worlds: one that actually is, and one that our mind has created. Reality and perception.

Perception... Oh, we give it so much power over us. It controls how we go about our lives. We blame it for our happiness, joy, sorrow, anxiety, sadness, bitterness, anger, shame, surprise, pride, embarrassment, boredom, satisfaction, and loneliness.

As time passes in our lives, we become more and more aware of these feelings that we have created. The days go by, and some of us wake up and realize that we do indeed have control over the world that our mind has generated.

We learn that the only thing that we can control in our lives is our reactions. If we want to be happy and joyful and compassionate, we have to consciously look for those little things in every moment. Seek them out. Look for the good in every situation.

The opposite is also true. If you constantly find yourself in a state of aggravation, boredom, bitterness, and aggression, it is your fault.

You have the power to change your future, and you have the fuel to do it now. Take a breath in and ask yourself, *What kind of life do I want to live?*

I believe that the key to living a joyful life is to have a heart filled with gratitude. When you look for things to be grateful for, you will see that you have SO MUCH to be grateful for. Write those things down. Seek them out. Smile. Thank God.

Know that this universe that we live in is so much bigger than we are. God has plans for us that are good and doesn't plan to harm us. You always need to keep that in your mind and in your heart. The world is not out there to piss you off. That is not why it was created.

My dear friends, your life is such a miracle. Look for the good. Be grateful for the good. Smile at the million little things that come before you each day and be grateful for them. Receive everything that happens to you with grace and acceptance. Being grateful increases your joy and lifts you above your circumstances.

Here's a list of things I'm grateful for:

The gentle heaving of my dog's chest as she sleeps cuddled next to me.

The smell of morning coffee being made.

The way my heart aches when my love is not around.

The smile of a passing stranger.

The wind that blows through the trees and the sound that

it creates.

The warmth of sunshine upon my shoulders.

The sweat and later soreness of a good workout.

The rain that hits the ground before me as I sit c o m - fortably on the porch.

The sizzle and smell of my dinner as it is being lovingly prepared.

The comfort that I feel when I hug my love.

The simple fact that I am forgiven and free.

My mother's laugh.

My father's stories.

My brother's smile.

Life is so wonderful when you realize that life is so wonderful.

Shout for joy to the Lord, all the earth.

Worship the Lord with gladness;

come before him with joyful songs.

Know that the Lord is God.

It is he who made us, and we are his[a];

we are his people, the sheep of his pasture.

Enter his gates with thanksgiving

The Storm

and his courts with praise;

give thanks to him and praise his name.

For the Lord is good and his love endures forever;

his faithfulness continues through all generations.

— PSALM 100, NIV

Praise be to the God and Father of our Lord Jesus Christ, who has blessed us in the heavenly realms with every spiritual blessing in Christ.

— EPHESIANS 1:3, NIV

Chapter 39: Finding the Good

It's probably easy to think about all of the hundreds--if not thousands--of things that are missing from your life when you've lost them. With the pandemic or an economic downturn, you might've given up ever having those things again like good health, good jobs, or happy relationships, and now you've settled into your "new normal." Some of you have let the darkness enter your soul and have found yourselves concentrating on and pining for the things you used to have or do.

You have become focused on your current situation's negativity, and it is stirring a deep, dark seed of discontent within you. You might be bitter and angry, and you may even refuse let any joy into your life "until this is all fixed."

I will bet you, though, if you change your mindset to one of gratitude and thanksgiving, this tough time can have a greater meaning... a greater outcome than your mind has ever imagined. Like my mom used to say, "You are just gonna have to make the best of it."

We might not be able to change our situation, but we CAN change our minds and attitudes--no matter what is before us. When you take nothing for granted, you will see that

The Storm

EVERYTHING is a blessing. You can find good in every situation. Although this might seem like an impossible feat right now, I promise you that it is simpler than you think.

God has given us the strength to do so much more than we would ever imagine. We should never worry about how we will get through the day because worrying about that is such a waste of our precious energy. His strength, through us, gives us what we need every day.

The sun has risen (and the Son will rise!).

We are alive.

We have salvation. Sunshine. Flowers. Air to breathe.

The grass (at least here in Texas) is green, and the birds are singing.

Most of us have spent more time with our immediate families than ever before during the pandemic. We have spent precious time with children and our spouses. We have played games, watched movies, completed household chores together. You, most likely, have spent the highest amount of quality family time EVER together. You have cooked together, laughed together, snuggled together, gone on long walks together. Talked more than ever before.

I bet one day, when your kids get older, they will look back at this time with a positive lens because they will smile and remember all of the time that was spent together being a family.

Or maybe you've been alone, and you might have realized that this is possibly the ONLY TIME you might have in your whole life to really get to know YOU. You have a journal to write. A meditation to perform. An exercise to do. A recipe you have always wanted to try. A friend to call. Take this time and work on yourself.

There weren't the million other "things" to do that used to pull us from what was most important. Maybe all of those "fillers" that we used to have in our lives really weren't that necessary. Maybe, by now, you have realized what is. I hope you do.

We cannot change what is going on all around us, no matter what may be going on in the world. We can only change our response to what is. If you only focus on the negative, you are cheating yourself. You are cheating God.

Whenever you find your mind going in the wrong direction, stop. Train yourself to look around and count the forty-five trillion things that are positive about whatever situation you are in. Open your eyes and look around... I mean REALLY open your eyes and take a look at what is around you. There is so much out there--right in front of your face--to be thankful for.

No matter what, you can choose to have every day centered not in disgust, but in gratitude, which will change you from the inside-out.

> I thank Christ Jesus our Lord, who has given me strength to do his work. He considered me trust-

worthy and appointed me to serve him.

— **TIMOTHY 1:12, NLT**

For this is how God loved the world: He gave his one and only Son, so that everyone who believes in him will not perish but have eternal life. God sent his Son into the world not to judge the world, but to save the world through him.

— **JOHN 3:16-17, NLT**

Chapter 40: God Is a Talkin' to Me!

A few years ago, I broke both of my ankles while hiking in Costa Rica. While the circumstances that led up to it all happening could have been a whole book in itself (let's just say it involved a swarm of wasps and a 6.7 magnitude earthquake), what happened **after** my accident was actually the much better story.

This is the story of getting close to my father...and my Father.

I have very vivid (and sometimes funny) dreams. I remember most of them in detail. That is also when God talks to me.

My trip home from Costa Rica was really horrible. I remembered crying the entire time on the plane because I was in so much pain. I didn't have my casts on yet. I was just wrapped in the ACE bandages all of the way up to my knees. I could not walk on my own feet and could only go in a wheelchair.

My father came down from Buffalo to help take care of me. That Monday, I found out that I had broken both of my ankles. I was going to be in double casts and in a wheelchair for a long, long time.

The Storm

I was really, really angry. I became the ultimate jerk because I believed that my freedom had been taken away. I treated my father awfully, even though he was just trying to help me. I was upset with my situation, and I took it out on him.

A little background information for you: my dad and I had kind of a turbulent past. Our relationship could be a little tumultuous at times when I was younger. He and I weren't close when I was growing up. As time has passed, dad and I have worked on our relationship a lot since those days, and we are really very close now, which is awesome.

I had a major pity party for myself. I lost all of my independence, and someone had to take care of me. I didn't like it one bit. I could not do ANYTHING (that was what it felt like, but it was really only partly true). Close your eyes and picture yourself for a moment with two casts on your legs. Think about any daily activity and imagine what could and could not be done with casts on both legs. It stunk big time.

Once particular night, during the epitome of me feeling sorry for myself, I snapped at my dad when he tried to move my pillow under my legs. I cried myself to sleep that night because I no longer was self-reliant. I was really such a jerk. All I could think about was everything I could not do, and my attitude just got worse and worse.

I finally fell asleep. Then I began to dream. God had something important to tell me.

All I remember was being in the dark and hearing a voice. I wasn't scared or anything, I felt at peace. The voice said, "Jennifer, you had become too independent. I am fixing that for you right now. Now is the time to be dependent on your Father. Let Him take care of you. Enjoy your time and build your relationship with your Dad. Don't waste this precious time."

And then I understood.

I woke up crying that morning. This time, it was a cry of joy. I called my dad in, and I told him that I was sorry and that I was so appreciative of him coming to my rescue when I needed him the most. From that day on, our relationship flourished. I enjoyed every minute of him being there and let him help me. I also worked on my relationship with my other Father.

When I acknowledged my neediness, I grew closer to both of my Fathers. I thanked God for this difficult time because through it, I realized my insufficiency was the key to further developing our relationship. Along the way, I discovered all of the beautiful things around me. My injury was a gift, and I was thankful for the powerful lesson. God just had His own way of showing me so that I would actually listen.

My attitude, along with my entire disposition, changed that morning. It also served an additional important lesson about mindset that I have carried with me--your gratitude fixes your attitude. My level of happiness shot up a trillion points that day, not because my experience changed...but because how I looked at it changed.

Thank you, Jesus.

Let the peace of Christ rule in your hearts, since as members of one body you were called to peace. And be thankful.

— COLOSSIANS 3:15, NIV

You will be enriched in every way so that you can be generous on every occasion, and through us your generosity will result in thanksgiving to God.

— 2 CORINTHIANS 9:11, NIV

Chapter 41: Comparison Is the Thief of Joy. For Reals, People.

The title of this chapter is one of my favorite "in yo face" quotes because it's so dang true! Teddy Roosevelt was a cool dude.

Why do we do compare? We look at what other people are doing (like on Facebook or any social media) and compare it to what we are doing, to how we are feeling. Ugh. Instant contentment killer.

Most women, when another woman walks into a room, do a complete comparison between them and her, and her mood can completely change because of this. When someone else does something really cool, instead of being happy for them, we think, "I deserve to do that too... what makes her/him so special?"

We see a movie, read a magazine, we see people who look better than us, have more than we do, and we compare. I wish I had that watch... I wish my butt was that small... my face that beautiful... That house is amazing compared to the one that I live in... etc., etc. We rob ourselves of so much joy.

Comparison is the thief of joy.

The Storm

One of the most important lessons I have learned over the years is this: *I am not everyone else*. I am not like everyone else. I don't WANT to be like anyone else. I am not going to do what everyone else is doing. I am just going to do my own thing. Who really cares what everyone else thinks? Stand out. Don't fit in.

My gifts are different than yours. We were all born with God-given gifts, and they are definitely not all of the same. We should embrace our differences and appreciate them versus comparing them to what others have because that comparison robs us of being grateful for what we DO have.

Instead of focusing on the things I don't have, I have changed my mindset to be grateful for what I have been given in this life. Even when I have nothing. My day begins with writing in my gratitude journal. When you focus on your blessings, something cool happens--the rest of the stuff doesn't matter. I don't give a care if you are skinnier than me or prettier than I am... I am my own person, and I am good with myself.

Now, don't get me wrong here. I do certainly look at what other people are doing and what they have, and sometimes that motivates ME to do better at something because I see that they can do it. But that's very different than comparing myself to them and letting it rob my joy. I have been enlightened enough to know that I don't know everything that has happened in their lives to get them where they are today. All I know is ME. *What am I doing? What have I been blessed with?*

If you have more than I do, that's awesome. I am good with what I have. If I want more or if I want to make a change in my life, it's because of MY decision--not because I have compared myself to you.

Likewise, you have to focus on what makes YOU unique instead of wishing you were someone else. Make a list of the amazing things about you. Start a gratitude journal to focus on what blessings you do have. Realize that when comparison rears its ugly head, you're comparing yourself to an unrealistic target.

You can't measure your life against someone else's. Geesh, you won't ever be happy if you do that! I guarantee you that you are so much more gifted than you think you are right now. So much more blessed than you feel right now. So much more beautiful than you believe you are. Count your blessings, and who cares about what everyone else has.

For we dare not number ourselves, or compare ourselves, with some who commend themselves. For in measuring themselves by themselves, and comparing themselves among themselves, they are not wise.

— 2 CORINTHIANS 10:12, 21ST CENTURY KJV

The Storm

Now about the gifts of the Spirit, brothers and sisters, I do not want you to be uninformed. You know that when you were pagans, somehow or other you were influenced and led astray to mute idols. Therefore I want you to know that no one who is speaking by the Spirit of God says, "Jesus be cursed," and no one can say, "Jesus is Lord," except by the Holy Spirit.

There are different kinds of gifts, but the same Spirit distributes them. There are different kinds of service, but the same Lord. There are different kinds of working, but in all of them and in everyone it is the same God at work.

Now to each one the manifestation of the Spirit is given for the common good. To one there is given through the Spirit a message of wisdom, to another a message of knowledge by means of the same Spirit, to another faith by the same Spirit, to another gifts of healing by that one Spirit, to another miraculous powers, to another prophecy, to another distinguishing between spirits, to another speaking in different kinds of tongues, and to still another the interpretation of tongues. All these are the work of one and the same Spirit, and he distributes them to each one, just as he determines.

— CORINTHIANS 12:1-11, NIV

Chapter 42: Eyes that See

Have we made the world so familiar that we don't really see it anymore? I think a lot of us do.

We go through our daily lives with blinders on, and we don't take the time to really look at what we see all around us. You see, our eyes are so powerful. The windows to and into the soul. The beauty in the world. God's wonders. What a blessing it is to have eyes that can see this spectacular world we live in.

Even with all of this amazingness around us, most of us totally miss it because we aren't being mindful of the present moment that we're in right now. And now... and now.

I'm thinking back to earlier that day and how I was feeling. I was sick, miserable, and headed to the doctors. There was a flurry of contractors at my house working feverishly on my bathroom. I drove to the doctors and then drove home. Sat on my chair and worked on projects. Just a day. Too sick to go to work. Nothing special. Pretty melancholy. Blah. Bored. Sick of sitting around doing nothing.

Then, I thought about all of the things that I really saw all around me then: hard work, kindness, frustration, love of the dogs, each dog's reaction to all of these people going in and out of the house while mom is home, barking at some and then wanting to be petted by others, frustration, helpfulness, love of God. My team had completely pulled together on the busiest day of the month without me. There was stress, joy, sickness, sadness, and exhaustion.

Now that's a lot of things to truly see! The interesting thing is that I really could have "seen" my day two very different ways as described above. You see, we see what we want to see, and we steer clear of what we don't. I wonder, *how much are we really limiting ourselves by "controlling" what we see?*

If you're scared, you will see things that affirm that you are scared. You can think of a million things that startled you, but you won't remember the kind man you talked to at the store.

Are you one who envies? Do you look at just the labels on everything and covet what you see? You can't remember the conversation that you just had with your sister while she was right next to you, but you know she had a Gucci belt on.

Are you judgmental? Are you always looking for what is wrong with everyone else?

Are you angry? You go through your day talking about those who have wronged you.

Unsure of yourself? You walk with your head down, and all you see is the ground.

Feel superior to everyone? All you can see is how much better you are than everyone you come in contact with. It is all you can talk about. Everyone is so stupid.

Or are you loving and compassionate? These are the people who live in the moment. They "see" the others and the world in the way that was described in the second paragraph of the recount of my day.

Most people who don't "see" let some negative emotion dictate how they really identify with the world around them. This negativity is easy stoppable if they recognize that's how they're seeing and choose right then and there to live in the present moment and see differently. It is only then they can feel the loving and compassionate viewpoint. When you stop dictating how you will see the world, you will find that you will actually have to stop and smell the roses. It is that simple.

So here's the thought: start listening to yourself when you talk. What are the conversations you are having actually saying about yourself? Do you talk over and over about the guy who cut you off and everyone else that wronged you that day? Or do you talk about how worried you are about everything? Do you talk about how everyone around you is an idiot? Are you too afraid to talk to people? They make you nervous. Do you explode in anger in conversations and talk about how everyone is out to make your life miserable? Do you want to buy every single designer thing you see on someone else, and you won't shut up about it?

The Storm

If you sound like that, then, Houston, you got a problem. You are not living in the moment. You have your blinders on. You are missing out in a truly authentic life filled with so much more than you are experiencing right now.

When we take the time to take in our surroundings and look for positive things, everything about you will change (And this is the stuff that wakes me up at 3 a.m. Ha).

> For in the same way you judge others, you will be judged, and with the measure you use, it will be measured to you.
>
> **— MATTHEW 7:2, NIV**

> A gentle answer deflects anger, but harsh words make tempers flare.
>
> **— PROVERBS 15:1, NLT**

Chapter 43: Grace Lenses

Imagine how amazing it would be if we could just put on some "grace lenses" and see ourselves as God sees us.

Now THAT would be cool--getting to see everyone, including ourselves, just as He does when He looks at us. We could see forgiveness and unconditional love. We would see sons and daughters of the Most High wherever we went. We should sense the spirits of love, power, and self-control. We would notice holy hearts, compassion, kindness, humility, and patience. The world would be so bright.

Imagine with me for a moment a world filled with people who had "grace lenses" on and just how different everything would be if we all looked at each other with love and delight. Looking through eyes of grace, we would be able to focus on the good and right versus the opposite like many of us do now.

The way you look at things is so powerful. It shapes your ENTIRE life because perception becomes your reality. There's a huge connection between the way we look at things and what we actually discover about our lives and the lives of others.

When we look at ourselves and others with "grace lenses," we discover eternal surprises that we never noticed before. Adoration, happiness, joy, acceptance, forgiveness, freedom, understanding, empathy, and unconditional love are just some of the things that we could recognize within us that really were there all along. They are just waiting to be revealed.

So maybe today we do something a little different... put those lenses on and focus on the good. See what happens.

The Spirit himself testifies with our spirit that we are God's children.

— ROMANS 8:16, NIV

For it is by grace you have been saved, through faith—and this is not from yourselves, it is the gift of God— not by works, so that no one can boast.

— EPHESIANS 2:8-9, NIV

Chapter 44:
Quarantined at Home

I get it. You have to be "stuck" in your home for a while. I have been there. Heck, I am still here now. It's easy to fall into the pit of thinking that you are missing out on the old life you had, maybe just a few days ago. Everyone is having fun, and you are shut in at home or in the hospital doing a bunch of nothing. The devil LOVES when you wallow in your negative thoughts. He will sit with you and feed them to you if you let him.

Your challenge today is to look at the positive things that come with staying at home. Let's focus on some positive things that come from you having to be isolated:

- You slowed down.

- You realized what was truly important.

- You now understand that relationships mean so much more than you ever thought.

- You ate dinner with your family... probably way more than you ever had before.

- You looked to God for help and strength.

- You spent time with your children and got to

know them.

- You got to know yourself.
- You realized how many silly things we fill our days up with that are meaningless.
- All of those thousand errands that you used to believe you had to run each week really aren't THAT important. Spending quality time with those you love is way better.
- You appreciate others so much more.
- Your gratitude increased.
- You paid attention to how your actions affected other people and became less selfish.

My prayer for those that are reading this is:

May you not lose hope.

Pick your head up and look forward.

Know that whatever is happening to you financially, you have the ability to climb out.

You can do this.

You cannot give up.

You must be strong and discerning when it comes to listening to those who are trying to limit you. You are much stronger than you think you are. Trust me.

Remember your resiliency.

Don't let your fear win.

Smile.

Be kind and generous to others.

Reach out to someone who might be hurting. Let someone else know when you are hurting.

Look for ways to brighten someone else's day.

Look people in the eye and acknowledge them when you see them.

Be human.

Turn off the news for a while and spend time with those who are in your home. You might not ever get this opportunity again.

If you're alone in your home, reach out to those you love to spend quality time listening and talking to them.

Believe in the goodness of others and your community. Together, you will rebuild.

Know that this shall pass.

You are never truly alone… God is right there with ya… so talk to Him. Build that relationship.

May God bless you in your journey today and always. Amen

> And now, dear brothers and sisters, one final thing. Fix your thoughts on what is true, and honorable, and right, and pure, and lovely, and admirable.

The Storm

Think about things that are excellent and worthy of praise.

— **PHIL. 4:8, NLT**

And we know that God causes everything to work together for the good of those who love God and are called according to his purpose for them.

— **ROMANS 8:28, NLT**

Chapter 45: Prayers Unanswered

I have heard that the greatest prayer unanswered is the prayer never prayed. I disagree.

I think the greatest prayer unanswered is one that was, but we weren't ready. I have learned that when you pray, you HAVE to believe in God's great power to make it happen. If you pray for rain, you had better prepare your fields. Trust His will. If it IS His will, then it's gonna happen. End of story.

BUT you have to also believe that it will happen. We have to make sure we are ready for it to happen. After all, we can't be asking God to do something in our lives and then not believe enough in Him to follow through.

You want to be healed? Prepare yourself to be healed. Change your mindset. Change your attitude. Be open-minded. Prepare.

You want to find love? Get your home in order. Get your thoughts together and make yourself ready so that when the prayer is answered for you, you are totally equipped for this person to love you back.

Do you want to heal from hurt? Then get your heart right.

Forgive. Open your soul so that the blessing of healing can be received.

You see? We pray these prayers to God to change certain things in our lives, but we don't take the necessary steps to lay the groundwork to receive the answers.

God has all of these plans for us. He says, "For I know the plans I have for you, plans to prosper you and not to harm you, plans to give you hope and a future" (Jeremiah 29:11, NIV).

How unfortunate it would be, my dear friends, to miss these amazing blessings because we didn't prepare for them to actually happen.

> No discipline seems pleasant at the time, but painful. Later on, however, it produces a harvest of righteousness and peace for those who have been trained by it.
>
> — HEBREWS 12:11, NIV

> Heal me, Lord, and I will be healed; save me and I will be saved, for you are the one I praise.
>
> — JEREMIAH 17:14, NIV

Chapter 46: The Shape of Me

My gratitude journal asked me a question yesterday that really got me thinking. The question was, "What is an experience that you are grateful for in your life that has shaped you into who you are today?"

Dang, gratitude journal, that is some deep stuff to ask a girl at 4:30 a.m.

I sat there and thought about it. Overwhelmingly, the things that I thought of were due to some of the darkest moments in my life.

Failure. Disappointment. Suffering. Distress. Tough times. These times in my life, even though they sucked while I was going through them, shaped me into who I am at this very moment... and for that, I am grateful. Through these uncomfortable moments, I was able to grow the most. Being "pruned" so that I could flourish.

My friends, failure is a GOOD thing. It means you have courage, guts, grit, and when you are going through hard times, remember that they are most likely temporary and that they WILL pass. When the difficulty is over, you're going to have a choice: will you learn and grow from your scars, or will you become bitter? THAT is the stuff that shapes you. What kind of person do you want to become? One who grows from the pruning or one who shrivels up and dies on the inside?

This topic isn't just about us, but it spills into how we parent, too. So many parents are afraid to let their kids fail or go through tough times. They want their children to only have good experiences in their lives without having any negative experiences. They want to do everything in their power to make sure their kids don't have to worry about anything. For the love of God, please stop that! You're hurting them worse by doing this. Let them fly on their own and make their own ways. Let them fail. It will make them better people, my dear friends.

The world is mysterious and unpredictable, and it's so easy to look at what is happening all around us and become discouraged and fearful. We don't wanna go through the times of adversity. Of course we don't! But, dang it--I promise you that you can come out so much stronger when you are out of that storm. Let the hard times shape you instead of destroying you.

God doesn't promise us a life full of butterflies and roses. He promises us that He will be right there, next to us, when we go through that valley. *Don't be afraid, for I am with you. I will strengthen you and help you.*

Here's a cheat sheet for how to reframe your viewpoint when it feels like things aren't going your way:

Adversity = Stronger You

Distress = Temporary

Failure = You have courage. Dust yourself off, get your butt, and get back up.

Hurt= Pruning

Suffering = Strength

Disappointment = Learning

Experiences = The shape of YOU

> When you go to battle against those who hate you and see more horses and war-wagons and soldiers than you have, do not be afraid of them. For the Lord your God, Who brought you from the land of Egypt, is with you.
>
> **— DEUTERONOMY 20:1, NLV**

> The Lord showed Himself to Isaac that same night, and said, "I am the God of your father Abraham. Do not be afraid, for I am with you. I will bring good to you, and add many to the number of your children and their children's children, because of My servant Abraham."
>
> **— GENESIS 26:24, NLV**

Chapter 47: Morning Routines

Having morning routines improves your life. Notice that I didn't say "could" or "might" improve your life. It WILL.

Sure, getting up at 4:30-5:00 a.m. every morning (except on the weekends, unless my body magically wakes up at that time) is tough sometimes because it is just so much easier to lay in bed all nice and warm... but I get up anyway. I don't ever regret it. Ever.

It is just like working out. There has never been one day that I have regretted getting up early AFTER I have actually done it. It is the "getting there" part that I struggle with sometimes.

My morning routine consists of me rising and making myself a cup of amazing coffee. I sit in my chair and have all of my books and my journals next to me on the table at arm's reach. There, I sit and read, pray, journal, think of the things--specific things--that I am grateful for. I do this for a good hour.

Then I go to the bathroom (ha, ha you just got TMI). This is real life, people. Real life.

Then I work out for an hour-ish before I take my shower and get ready for the day that is in front of me. I don't get to work until 9:00 a.m. So before I even go to work, I have been up and productive for almost five hours.

Today, I am going to hone-in a little on the first hour of the morning--the time for prayer and meditation and what that does.

Spending time with God is part of my morning routine. Simply put, this is the best hour of my entire day. It is the most important. It is the most powerful. I think about gratitude and how God is working in my life, then I read His Word and meditate about whatever is on my heart that morning. This is the most paramount part of the day.

My mind is clears, and my heart opens. Thoughts unscramble. *I am ready to hear what You have to say to me, God.*

Thinking of things I am grateful for--specific things-- has, in turn, made me even MORE grateful for the beautiful life that I lead. It is really cool how that works: the more grateful you are, the more you realize just how many things you have to be grateful for.

Sometimes I love what He puts on my heart. At other times, He tells me something that I don't necessarily want to hear about. A change I need to make or something that I should do. I pray for people, I pray to be a light in the world, and I pray for direction. I pray that He shows me the true hearts of the people in my life. Sometimes I don't love what He reveals... and that is OKAY. I have learned that when a door is shutting for me, there is something so much better in store.

Spending this precious hour clears the day ahead of me. It removes obstacles I thought I had and helps to put me on a straight path. This path might not necessarily be the one that I had intended, but that really doesn't matter. I learned long ago that in the end, it is not up to me at all. So now I just go with it.

He gives me insights and glimpses of the life He wants me to lead.

And I listen. This is something that I have struggled with in the past... the actual listening part. Even when I hear Him loud and clear, sometimes I don't truly listen. Then I don't take action either. I want to go my own way and on my own path because *I know what I'm doing.* We know how that all turns out. I have definitely gotten so much better at the taking action part also. Even when I don't want to (in my mind). I know His way is so much better.

This way, my day starts peacefully and without all of the frazzle and rushing around. It is beautiful, and I hope that I will continue to do this throughout all of the days of my life. Early rising is so much better than waking up at the last second and rushing to get ready for work or getting the kids ready for school, etc.

This simple morning routine has changed my life. It will for you, too. Maybe you're not an early bird (side note: I was not originally, but I became one over time), but with practice, you can be. You will soon wonder how in the heck you survived all of those years NOT waking up early. You will discover that there is so much more to life than sleeping till the last second before you have to do something. You will cherish this time, and it will become the best part of your day. Probably the most productive too!

Turn off the TV. Put your phone down. Go to bed.

Wake up early and spend time with yourself and with God in solitude before anyone else in your house wakes up.

There's plenty of time for everything else. You just gotta do it.

> But as for me, I will sing about your power. Each morning I will sing with joy about your unfailing love. For you have been my refuge, a place of safety when I am in distress.
>
> **— PSALM 59:16, NLT**

> Let me hear of your unfailing love each morning, for I am trusting you. Show me where to walk, for I give myself to you.
>
> **—PSALM 143:8, NLT**

> For wisdom will enter your heart,
>
>   and knowledge will fill you with joy.

Morning Routines

Wise choices will watch over you.

Understanding will keep you safe.

—PROVERBS 2:10-11, NLT

Chapter 48: A Lesson from a Zit

Yesterday, I noticed a small pimple on my shoulder. For reals, it was tiny. I immediately put some medicine on it and covered it up with my shirt so that no one could see my "imperfection." Perhaps even weirder was the fact that I was the only one home, so no one else was going to see it anyway. *Just in case.*

Every single time I got up and walked past ANY mirror, I checked out my blemish. I focused on it. I even said out loud, "I can't believe I have a stupid zit on my shoulder." Several times! I literally obsessed about this stupid little thing that I found wrong with me. An imperfection.

Am I really that vain? What the heck's wrong with me, and why am I obsessing over this ridiculously small spot?

'Cause that's what a lot of women do (men, pay attention here because I am going to give you some woman insight here, and how we think!). Oh, I know I am not alone here. Don't even TRY and deny it! We focus on our "defects," and we let them control what we do and how we act WAY all-too-often. Instead of focusing on the good and beautiful parts of ourselves, we brood over the things that are wrong with us. Rather than loving ourselves just as we are, we nitpick and find the things that we detest, and then try and hide them so that no one else will see the REAL us. Yikes!

Then you have my fiancé who could have the most giant zit on his back--I mean, one the size of Mt. Kilimanjaro--and it would not stop him from whipping off his shirt in front of everyone to go swimming (the mayhem!). He doesn't care. He would not ever let an imperfection like that stop him from living his life, let alone control what he does.

I am not gonna lie, there have been times when I have not gone somewhere because of a zit on my face or something else I was unhappy with about myself. If I felt fat... bloated... didn't like my hair that day... blah, blah, blah. I am not proud of these feelings and actions, which seem even more ridiculous now that I am typing them out (because they are!). *What a waste. I missed out.*

And this, my lady friends, is a lesson we need to learn from men. We need to stop obsessing over our "imperfections."

We are beautiful. Most likely (especially if it is someone who loves you), no one will even notice the "shortcomings" that you think you have because they love you for YOU. We need to love ourselves in that same way.

No one is perfect. It is part of being human.

Love your scars. Love your pimples. Embrace the parts of you--inside and out--that you're not so happy with. Love your imperfect selves. It is all good. The world will go on, and no one will give a crap about your so-called blemish.

When Michael got home yesterday, I didn't have any make-up on, and my hair had naturally dried. I wasn't the "best version of myself" in my mind. One of the first things he said to me was how naturally beautiful he thought that I was.

He didn't notice my pimple.

> Now we see things imperfectly, like puzzling reflections in a mirror, but then we will see everything with perfect clarity. All that I know now is partial and incomplete, but then I will know everything completely, just as God now knows me completely.
>
> — 1 CORINTHIANS 13:12, NLT

> For you know that it was not with perishable things such as silver or gold that you were redeemed from the empty way of life handed down to you from your ancestors, but with the precious blood of Christ, a lamb without blemish or defect.
>
> — 1 PETER 1:14-18, NIV

Chapter 49: Sunbeams and Dust

I love the morning sunshine that beams its way into my house in the morning. It is so peaceful to see it. It makes me smile. The warmth of the sunbeams penetrates my home and bring me joy and peace...

Until it very clearly highlights every single speck of dust in my house, and I cringe. I now see the flaws in my house. Dirt. Dust. Imperfections. Bleck! My first inclination is to stop everything I'm doing and clean, but then my mind kindly asks me, *Why did you do that? You ruined our moment.*

Good question. Why DO we look at something so beautiful and tear it apart so that we only see its flaws? I self-sabotaged what should have been a very beautiful moment that God created. It WAS perfect, until I CHOSE to see its defects. It wasn't supposed to be that way.

As women especially, we do this every day. We look at our beautiful selves and hone-in on the minuscule imperfections that we have and turn them into big things. We cringe when we look at them. We stop seeing our exquisiteness and splendor--the qualities we REALLY have--and instead focus on tiny "deficiencies" that we have magnified in our minds.

Rather than embracing the inherent beauty that is with

all of us, we hide. We take a moment that is meant to be so beautiful and obstruct and ravage its appeal with criticism.

As people, we don't take the time out of our days to appreciate the beautiful things and moments that come before us. Instead, we think about all of the things that went "wrong" in our day.

My wish for today is this:

That we take time to cherish those small moments in our days where there is beauty and peace.

That we start looking for things that are right instead of imperfections.

That we realize that we are God's children, and He made us. We are beautiful. Embrace our magnificence.

That we focus on what is good, true, right, noble, pure, and lovely. THOSE are the things we should be thinking about.

If our minds start to wander, that we quickly recognize our negative thinking and put an end to it. Immediately.

That we stop sabotaging those beautiful moments that God has created. Pause. Appreciate. Smile. Love.

May we BE the lights to others in this world.

That when we see something that IS beautiful in someone else, we tell them.

It is that simple.

Sunbeams and Dust

How priceless is your unfailing love, O God! People take refuge in the shadow of your wings.

— PSALM 36:7, NIV

Finally, brethren, whatever things are true, whatever things are noble, whatever things are just, whatever things are pure, whatever things are lovely, whatever things are of good report, if there is any virtue and if there is anything praiseworthy—meditate on these things.

—PHILIPPIANS 4:8, KJV

Chapter 50: Gratitude and Thanksgiving

God calls us to be thankful in ALL circumstances. It is really difficult to do this. He knows. He wants you to do it anyway. The joy that you get from practicing this daily far outweighs the effort that it takes to do it.

Gratitude transforms you. When you look for the good in all circumstances, your light shines brighter each day.

Take some time over the next few days and answer or complete the questions and tasks below. Then put them into practice, and you will see how much thanksgiving influences every aspect of your life.

Start a gratitude journal. This is an integral part that you must include in your transformation. It can be something as simple as a spiral notebook. Use it every day and write down specific things that you are thankful for. They can be simple things or stuff that is more monumental. It doesn't matter as long as you write them down, thank God for them, and smile. Write down five things you are grateful for right now.

_____

_____

_____

_____
_____
_____
_____

What are some good things in your life that you have taken for granted?

_____
_____
_____
_____
_____
_____
_____

Today, I want you to pay attention to all of the signs, coincidences, and your subconscious thoughts today. That is God talkin' to you! What is He saying?

_____
_____
_____
_____
_____
_____
_____
_____

_____
_____
_____
_____
_____

Do you find yourself consistently coveting what some-one else has? What kind of things do you desire?

_____
_____
_____
_____
_____

Let's focus on what you do have. Write down ten things that makes you... well, YOU.

_____
_____
_____
_____
_____
_____
_____
_____
_____
_____

_____

_____

_____

What do you have to be joyful about?

_____

_____

_____

_____

_____

_____

Think about your day today. It may have seemed frustrating at times, but what did you REALLY see? List out all of the good things that you may have missed.

_____

_____

_____

_____

_____

_____

_____

_____

_____

_____

Gratitude and Thanksgiving

_____

_____

_____

Today, put on your grace lenses and keep them on all day. Write about your experience and how things were different.

_____

_____

_____

_____

_____

_____

_____

_____

_____

_____

_____

_____

Write down some negative thoughts that you have had lately. At the end of the list, write, "These thoughts are not from God. They are from the devil. Get away from me, devil. I am not listening to you. I have Jesus with me, and He is all that I need. He takes away my burdens and carries them for me." It will feel great.

The Storm

_____

_____

_____

_____

_____

_____

_____

_____

_____

_____

_____

_____

_____

_____

_____

_____

_____

_____

_____

_____

Are you ready for the outcome of the prayers that you have petitioned for?

_____

_____

_____

_____

Gratitude and Thanksgiving

_____

_____

_____

If you have not properly prepared for God's answers for your prayers, what can you do now to show Him that you are ready to receive?

_____

_____

_____

_____

_____

_____

_____

Has failure and disappointment in your life shaped you into who you are today?

_____

_____

_____

_____

_____

_____

_____

_____

_____

The Storm

_____
_____
_____
_____
_____
_____

Do you have a daily routine? If so, write it out and why
it is important that you do as you do.

_____
_____
_____
_____
_____
_____
_____
_____
_____
_____

What are your mornings like?

_____
_____
_____
_____

_____

_____

_____

How could structure or getting up earlier help you with your day?

_____

_____

_____

_____

_____

_____

_____

Why aren't you doing it?

_____

_____

_____

Why is spending time with God so important?

_____

_____

_____

_____

_____

_____

_____

The Storm

Have you ever not gone somewhere because of your perception of an imperfection you have (Don't lie! I know you have)? What did you miss out on? Do you regret not going?

_____

_____

_____

_____

_____

_____

_____

What makes you beautiful/handsome?

_____

_____

_____

_____

_____

_____

What will you tell yourself next time you feel "imperfect?"

_____

_____

_____

_____

_____
_____
_____

Why do you think you look at your defects rather than the beautiful parts of yourself?

_____
_____
_____
_____
_____
_____
_____
_____
_____
_____
_____
_____
_____

Who can you call today to tell them they are beautiful or special? Do it, and journal how they reacted.

_____
_____
_____
_____

The Storm

_____

_____

_____

_____

_____

What can you do to be a light in the world?

_____

_____

_____

_____

_____

_____

PART 4:

Overcoming

Chapter 51: Where I Come From, You Have a Choice

At the age of forty-five, I feel like I have lived the life of a few people combined that are way further along than a mere forty-five years. Here's just the highlights:

I had an unstable childhood filled with abuse from an alcoholic parent.

I had bronchitis and strep throat almost monthly, well into my adulthood. You can throw a bunch of pneumonias in there also, peppered too frequently throughout the years.

Major surgery when I was fifteen (on my birthday) to remove a tumor the size of a football, along with my right ovary and appendix. Several subsequent abdominal surgeries to remove cysts. Untwisting of my fallopian tube a few times. Cutting of nerves.

I was raped when I was just thirteen by a man three times my age.

Triple fusion on my neck that didn't ever heal correctly.

Abusive physical relationship where I was assaulted and bitten by a crazy man.

Thyroid cancer and subsequent removal of my thyroid. Then, gaining over a hundred pounds as result and taking three years to lose that weight.

Went through the heartache of failed in-vitro twice and my embryos not making it on the day of implantation.

Tonsils out as an adult.

Pulmonary emboli (PE) and deep vein thrombosis (DVT) when I was twenty-four. DVT and, even worse, PE again just last month. I was recently diagnosed with a form of chronic obstructive pulmonary disease and pulmonary hypertension from my blood clots.

Breaking both ankles in a hiking accident. Having casts on both my legs for twelve weeks.

Attacked by wasps while in the midst of a 6.7 magnitude earthquake.

Being burglarized of everything in my home now twice over with devastating losses.

Major concussion from flipping over while tubing in the river where I completely and literally lost my mind for a few weeks.

Oh, and this weekend, I was stabbed by a stinkin' sting-ray in my foot and had to endure the unbelievable pain that the venom inflicts.

There are many more "things" that have happened to me,

but we don't have all day to go over them.

Let's just say, I can't make this stuff up! There's a lot.

And through it all, I've had a smile on my face. Despite that some of these things I listed should have definitely killed me for sure. *This girl is here for a reason.*

I have also beaten all of these maladies. I not only beat them, I kicked their stupid butts. I don't let them affect the life I live *right now.* I don't blame them for anything other than making me who I am. I come from a place of *overcoming*, so my advice comes from actually going through things, not just guessing what it was like. I LIVED it.

I have also summited Mt. Kilimanjaro, conquered Tour de Mont Blanc, and scaled Mt. Whitney. I have travelled throughout the world. I have helped make a difference in many lives. I have risen to the top in my field and have been the focus in numerous write ups and accolades. I have mentored others and learned to give freely to those who are in need. I have loved deeply. I have helped change lives. I made people laugh, cry, love, and think. I have forgiven and I have BEEN forgiven. I have brought people to Christ.

Through it all, I would NOT change one single thing.

Not even the stingray stab I got this weekend. If someone was supposed to have gotten stabbed, I'm happy to have been one to take it versus Michael, my husband, (it would have stopped him from being able to work) or his kiddos (so they didn't have to endure the pain). I am glad it was me instead of any one of them. Michael was my hero over the weekend as he took care of me once again. He even carried me up two flights of stairs because I could not walk. We laughed so hard at the situation that I was crying (because, well, it was hilarious; we were like, "REALLY??"), and we made funny videos of our account of my newest adventure.

You see, it is through all of these adversities that I became who I am... and I really love my life. I love the woman I have become. It is through my difficulties that I found myself. I found God. I found peace. I found joy. I appreciate life so much more than many others. I don't take things for granted. I savor my time. I smile a lot. I LIVE my life.

'Cause I know that God has a plan for me. He does for you too.

He took all of these bad things that happened, the things that would crush or kill most people, and He used them for good for me. Because I let Him. I didn't give up. God gave me the strength to conquer them all, and for that I am grateful. God knew that I could take it, and I have done so with grace, love and understanding. He can do the same for you.

Through my greatest sorrows, I have had the most joy. Through my greatest "knock downs," I have gotten up and become that much stronger. Through my greatest struggles, I have had the most amazing victories.

I cannot imagine the person I would be if I hadn't gone through all of these things. I am a better person for it all.

It's okay to get knocked down by life's circumstances, but the important thing--THE MOST IMPORTANT THING--is what you are going to do about it. Run and hide and be bitter? Angry? Have a pity party for yourself? Or face it head on, laugh, and know that *this too, shall pass*?

Would you rather live a life of "what ifs" or a life of "I went for it"? THAT is what diversity did for me. It propelled me to live the life of "I went for it," and man, it has been great.

There are so many people who just sit around and reminisce about things that they wish they could do or want to do. **Then there are people who DO.** Which one do you want to be?

You are fearfully and wonderfully made... so act like it.

We ALL have problems. So many people have had way worse things happen to them than we ever will. When these things happen, you have a choice, ONE choice, and that is your reaction.

You can choose to pause, smile, and accept your present situation. Know that God has got you. Find peace in the fight.

Or you can give up and be defeated.

It's up to you.

Finally, be strong in the Lord and in his mighty power. Put on the full armor of God, so that you can take your stand against the devil's schemes. For our struggle is not against flesh and blood, but against the rulers, against the authorities, against the powers of this dark world and against the spiritual forces of evil in the heavenly realms. Therefore put on the full armor of God, so that when the day of evil comes, you may be able to stand your ground, and after you have done everything, to stand. Stand firm then, with the belt of truth buckled around your waist, with the breastplate of righteousness in place, and with your feet fitted with the readiness that comes from the gospel of peace. In addition to all this, take up the shield of faith, with which you can extinguish all the flaming arrows of the evil one. Take the helmet of salvation and the sword of the Spirit, which is the word of God.

— EPHESIANS 6:10-17, NIV

Consider it pure joy, my brothers and sisters, whenever you face trials of many kinds, because you know that the testing of your faith produces perseverance. Let perseverance finish its work so that you may be mature and complete, not lacking anything. If any of you lacks wisdom, you should ask God, who gives generously to all without finding fault, and it will be given to you. But when you ask, you must believe and not doubt, because the one who doubts is like a wave of the sea, blown and tossed by the wind.

— 1 JAMES 1:2-7, NIV

Chapter 52: Becoming Weak to Become Strong

This past week, I went to the hematologist for my post-hospital care. I don't know what I was expecting, but I was pretty disappointed with the news I heard regarding what it will take for my recovery.

For the past ten years, I woke up between 4:30-5:00 a.m. with a routine: make coffee, read, pray, write, meditate for an hour, and then hit my gym for at least an hour. Fitness was a huge part of my life, and I absolutely loved working out. It made me feel better both mentally and physically. It was my stress relief, and I also loved how I looked when I am in great shape (yeah, I know it may sound shallow, but it was honest).

So, I was incredibly bummed when the doctor told me that because of the amount of clots I had in both of my legs, they were afraid of more clots breaking off and going into my lungs.

So, I have to be very careful. For the next three months, I cannot exert myself at all. That means no lifting weights, no long walks, no hiking, no squats... NOTHING for what will seem like forever.

I can increase my physical activity as time progresses,

but I'm walking on flat surfaces only, and that's about it. Then I can progress to five-pound weights (which, just a few days ago, would have been a complete joke). Right now, I can't do much of anything anyway, as I get winded just emptying the dang dishwasher.

There's just something psychological though that pains me when someone tells me that I can't do something for a while that I love to do. I know it's not permanent, but I immediately thought that all my hard work to get fit over the past ten years was all for naught. It made me both mad and sad. I had a little pity party for myself.

I immediately started worrying about when I did go back to work and the amount of stress that came with my career. *How would I handle it?* Exercise had been my answer to battling this issue.

I cried on Friday. A lot. I had a lot of soul-stirring going on. I felt like everything that I had been holding back emotionally just came out at once. I was scared. Mad. Happy to be alive. Thankful for everyone in my life that cares about me so much. I felt loved. Pissed at my body. Crushed. Guilty that my team has to do all of the work. Useless. Worried. Defeated. Joyful. You name it, I probably had that feeling on Friday.

The words that came to me over and over were this: **I have to let my body become weak in order to be strong again.** That is a hard thing for this girl to take. Pretty devastating actually. Truth be told, it depressed the heck out of me.

I made myself a sandwich for lunch. Out of breath once again, I sat down at the kitchen bar, and it came to me: that was what Jesus did. *He made Himself weak so that we could become strong, through Him.*

I just sat there and cried again. This time, it was different though. It was one of those, "Aha... OKAY, God, I get it" cries. Couldn't say this realization suddenly made me feel one hundred percent better, but it did put things into perspective a lot more. Sacrifice now to make things better in the end. This was part of His plan for me, and I knew that something amazing was going to come out of this.

This awareness doesn't make it any easier in the meantime though. As I am writing this, my emotions are stirring up again, and my Michael just came here and gave me a big, long hug. I told him what I was writing about, and he reminded me of something important that the doctor had said: my fitness is what saved my life. If I hadn't been in such good shape, I would be dead right now.

Another reminder that there is a reason for everything. God has already been preparing me for this moment.

Sometimes we wonder: why is this happening? What is the purpose? All of this hard work done for nothing.

So we think. Our human minds default too the negative all-too-often. Nonetheless, that is not how God works, and

you have to remember that, even when it makes no freakin'
sense to you. My mini meltdown ended up in a profound
understanding as to what I had unknowingly been preparing
for throughout the past ten years.

God knit all of those pieces together so that I would survive my storm. He will and has done the same for you. You
just have to trust Him. Talk to Him… and then listen.

> John is the man to whom the Scriptures refer when
> they say, 'Look, I am sending my messenger ahead
> of you, and he will prepare your way before you.'
>
> — MATTHEW 11:10, NLT

> But God demonstrates his own love for us in this:
> While we were still sinners, Christ died for us.
>
> — ROMANS 5:8, NIV

Chapter 53: 2 Miles and 5 Pound Weights/ Surviving Blood Clots Once Again/Learning to Listen Even When I Don't Wanna

Who would have thought that walking two miles with no incline would kick my butt and wear me out? My newly damaged lungs and tired body are a far cry from where they were just a few short months ago. It is challenging, this slowing down stuff. Taking it easy... I had forgotten what that actually meant until recently.

Mentally, it is difficult to take. It is weird not to feel like yourself, if that makes sense. My current life is very unlike the "old me." Slowed down a bit but feeling like a screeching halt, to say the least. My days now consist of puttering around the house and running a few errands. Too tired to do much else.

Every ache and pain brings me anxiety, and I find myself getting a little scared sometimes of the "what ifs" that go through my mind. What if I have another clot forming? Why does my leg hurt so bad? What is that pain in my back when I breathe? What if more of the ones I have break off and go into my lungs and damage them further or kill me this time? I constantly have to remind myself that I have to live in the present moment and stop thinking about the things that might happen in the future. What a waste of time that is, worrying about things that may or may not happen. The Bible talks about anxiety and worrying a lot too. Bottom line: Jen, stop being anxious.

Easy to say, harder to do. I know. I am doing it, though.

The good news is I now have a lot of reading and writing and time for reflection. That part has been nice. I have written my booty off, and I feel like God has given me some really great ideas and insight. For that, I am grateful.

I know there is a great reason for all of this, and I smile thinking about the WHY and the WHAT that is to come. A million possibilities ahead of me and a million miracles that have kept me alive through my now second bout with deep vein thrombosis (DVT) and pulmonary emboli (PE). I survived, once again, clots that were large enough to kill most everyone else.

You would think that I would absolutely know the warning signs of these blood clots, having had them before. In my defense, it has been about twenty years, so a girl can forget...

I found an old journal in my closet that I had written

back in 2001, when I had my first battle. I wrote everything down back then just like I do now! Convenient.

I started noticing that I got out of breath really easily. The shortness of breath progressed with time until just walking or talking completely winded me.

My "back" hurt a lot, like in the middle where my ribs are, and it felt like a pinched nerve. It really hurt when I tried to take a deep breath in, so I stopped doing that. The pain became more and more excruciating, and it was constant.

It hurt to lay down, and I found myself having to prop myself up to sleep. I had a charley horse in my leg, and it just felt tight, like there was a ton of pressure in my legs whenever I squatted down. The pain would not go away. I thought I had pulled a muscle from working out and lifting heavy weights.

I had crazy anxiety that I convinced myself was attributed to my work. My pulse was high--which I had falsely attributed to my high anxiety. 120 is NOT normal, Jen. Those were my symptoms back in 2001, which happened to be the same exact ones that I chose to ignore last month.

I feel so dumb as I write this. I mean, really... Jen, you have totally already been through this exact same scenario, and it was THE most difficult battle of your life. How did you not know?

I was in denial. Big time. Truth be told, I did see the

signs, and if you were to look through my Google search history, you would see that I did research blood clots and signs and symptoms. Still, I chose NOT to believe that this was actually happening to me once again. I said out loud many times, "I better not have another blood clot." I should have listened to my body.

Twenty years ago, I smoked, was overweight, and was on a heavy dose of birth control. A far, far cry from the shape that I am in now. *No way it would happen again.* Wrong.

Under normal circumstances, the "Jen of today" is an athlete. A trekker and hiker who turns into a crazy unstoppable machine as soon as she gets on a mountain trail. Working out six days a week with heavy weights was the norm.

Was, and will be once again with a lot of patience, Lord willing. The rebuilding stage has begun, and I know the road I have ahead of me. I am hoping my muscles have a photographic memory. Ha, ha.

I know that my current fitness level is what saved me. I had unknowingly been preparing for these days for many years. *Thank you, Lord.* Grandma's words that she had ingrained into my mind actually paid off: "Your health is your wealth." I got it, Gram. I took care of myself just like you wanted me to. It served me well and has kept me alive.

Listen to your body. You KNOW when there is something wrong. Don't ignore your inner voice because you are "too busy" to have something wrong with you! You might be too late.

When things like this happen to us, it's easy to say, "Why me?" It is easy to shake your fist at God and be so scared about what is next. What will it be like now? You're going to have to take things one day at a time... one precious moment at a time.

Uncertainty breeds anxiety. I know you might be scared right now. The "you" that you knew just a few days ago is not the same "you" as today. Life is different. You have a new normal right now. Your old self is no longer, and it is okay. Take this treasured time to do an assessment of your life.

Think about what kind of life you have led and pray about the changes you need to make in it. Maybe when all of this is over, the "old normal" will be long gone and replaced with something better and more meaningful. Maybe the path that you thought that you should be on was the wrong one the whole time. Now you're on a new path. I pray that God reveals the purpose of your suffering. In the meantime, use this time wisely, as you might not ever get this chance again.

Even when there was no reason for hope, Abraham kept hoping—believing that he would become the father of many nations. For God had said to him, "That's how many descendants you will have!"

— **ROMANS 4:18, NLT**

The Storm

No wonder my heart is glad, and my tongue shouts his praises! My body rests in hope.

— **ACTS 2:26, NLT**

And this hope will not lead to disappointment. For we know how dearly God loves us, because he has given us the Holy Spirit to fill our hearts with his love.

— **ROMANS 5:5, NLT**

Chapter 54: Out of Control

I know. I feel it, too. Right now, you feel like your world is out of control. Any sense of routine that you had grown to love has gone. The world around you is volatile, and that creates uncertainty, which creates some insecurity in your head. You're not the only one. There are lots of us.

When we are shaken out of our comfort zones into a new world of unfamiliarity, our first reaction might be to be angry or resentful of our current circumstance. Now is the time to take God's hand tightly and look for the positive ways that you can use this time to grow and change with the season you are in.

Instead of getting aggrieved with your situation, you have to change your mindset and look for the positive side of the environment of which you are now in. After all, you know that the ONLY thing that we can actually choose is our reactions to the things that happen to us. You are going to have to look at things a different way. Accept the change. Acknowledge it and welcome its challenge.

Through the pruning, we grow.

It is super easy right now to just throw your hands up and give up. To let yourself go. To stop giving a care. Right now is not the time to do that. You have been knocked down. Dust yourself off. Look up. Take God's hand and march forward.

Now is the time for you to decide who you want to be and how you want to react to the changes.

Now is the time to display your character and the fortitude you have to get through times that try every inch of your soul.

Now is the time to fight against the devil that whispers negativity in your ear.

Now is the time to get off your butt and get onto your knees and talk to God.

Now is the time to show everyone what you are made of. You have strength, grit, perseverance, faith, trust, love, and hope on your side. You are so much stronger and resilient than you think you are.

You are not alone.

I am the true vine, and my Father is the gardener. He cuts off every branch in me that bears no fruit, while every branch that does bear fruit he prunes so that it will be even more fruitful. You are already clean because of the word I have spoken to you. Remain in me, as I also remain in you. No branch can bear fruit by itself; it must remain in the vine. Neither can you bear fruit unless you remain in me.

Out of Control

I am the vine; you are the branches. If you remain in me and I in you, you will bear much fruit; apart from me you can do nothing. If you do not remain in me, you are like a branch that is thrown away and withers; such branches are picked up, thrown into the fire and burned. If you remain in me and my words remain in you, ask whatever you wish, and it will be done for you. This is to my Father's glory, that you bear much fruit, showing yourselves to be my disciples.

— JOHN 15:1-8, NIV

Chapter 55: The Armor of God

Satan has been probably whispering in your ear lately. Telling you that there isn't hope. You aren't strong enough to get through this chaos. You aren't going to make it. Go ahead and act badly, it's okay. Live on the dark side. Give up. Your world has gone down the tubes. It is never going to get better. You are in this for yourself only. Who cares what you do? Don't help anyone, only help yourself. Take that drink. Turn your head away from that person. Be selfish, you deserve it. Where is God in all of this? He abandoned you. Why even try? You won't make it. Join me.

Sound familiar? If you have found yourself getting discouraged, sad, anxious, worried, or if you have heard the whispers above... I want you to read this passage that is coming along with what I write after it:

The Armor of God

Finally, be strong in the Lord and in his mighty power. Put on the full armor of God, so that you can take your stand against the devil's schemes. For our struggle is not against flesh and blood, but against the rulers, against the authorities, against the powers of this dark world and against the spiritual forces of evil in the heavenly realms. Therefore put on the full armor of God, so that when the day of evil comes, you may be able to stand your ground, and after you have done everything, to stand. Stand firm then, with the belt of truth buckled around your waist, with the breastplate of righteousness in place, and with your feet fitted with the readiness that comes from the gospel of peace. In addition to all this, take up the shield of faith, with which you can extinguish all the flaming arrows of the evil one. Take the helmet of salvation and the sword of the Spirit, which is the word of God.

— EPH 6:10-17, NIV

The armor of God is a powerful tool against the lies you hear whispered in your ear. God gives us the ability to fight and stand out ground against the devil's schemes.

Take special notice about one detail that people tend to overlook in this passage: **There is nothing covering your backside.** There is no butt armor or back armor. WHY? Because you are supposed to run toward the fight instead of running away from it.

God equips us with what we need to tell the devil to get out of my face!!! To stand firm in truth, righteousness, love, peace, His Word, faith, hope, salvation. So dang it, do NOT give up. Know that God is with you, and He has equipped you to fight the fight through Him and WITH Him. You, my dear one, are going to be okay.

> But the Lord is faithful, and he will strengthen you and protect you from the evil one.
>
> **— 2 THESSALONIANS 3:3, NIV**

Chapter 56: Thankful for the Scars

I have a lot of scars. Both on my body and in my mind. I used to hate them, but now I am thankful for them.

Think about this... think about your scars... mental and physical. Think about how when you were going through whatever it was--how badly it sucked. Yeah, I know. But here's the cool thing: God was with you the whole entire time. Right next to you, holding you. You just had to open your eyes and heart to see, hear, and feel Him.

At this point in all of our lives, we ALL have scars, shame, doubts... but the one thing that you should never doubt is where God is during all of this. 'Cause He is right there. It is your choice, whether or not to feel that... but I will tell you that life will be much different if you get it.

My scars have changed me. They have shaped me. They have molded me into who I am today. They are my battle wounds that say, "Guess what, I won!"

So, the next time you look at yourself in the mirror and want to hate your scars on your body or in your mind or in your heart, look at them a different way...

They are proof that God is and was with you, and together you are tough as nails.

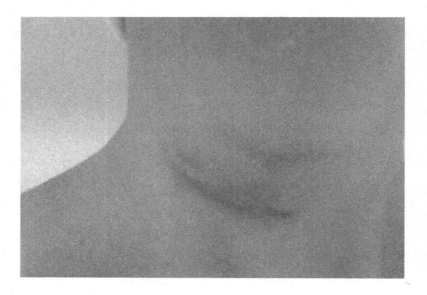

We can rejoice, too, when we run into problems and trials, for we know that they help us develop endurance. 4 And endurance develops strength of character, and character strengthens our confident hope of salvation. 5 And this hope will not lead to disappointment. For we know how dearly God loves us, because he has given us the Holy Spirit to fill our hearts with his love.

— ROMANS 5:3-5, NLT

From now on, don't let anyone trouble me with these things. For I bear on my body the scars that show I belong to Jesus.

— GALATIANS 6:17, NLT

Chapter 57: Living Your Best Life Now

I think we can all agree that each of our lives becomes the shape of the days we inhabit, right? Each day goes by-- one at a time--and then all of the sudden, BAM. You're forty, fifty, eighty...

One of the greatest sins is to have a life that has been "un-lived." We were born into this world with a million possibilities, and it is a shame how many people will express regret about not living the life they should have lived when they are on their deathbed thinking, "If I only had one more year, I would have done...."

Why do so many people do that? They let the days go by, one after another, and never live the life that they dream they could have. They listen to the barriers in their heads that limit them and tell them, "no."

Pause from reading for a minute. Think about the dreams that tug at your soul, the thoughts that come from your heart. Recognize the innate gifts that only YOU were born with. The wants you have and the endless possibilities before you that are meant to shape YOUR individual life (they are quite different than mine). What you are choosing to do with each day of your life that you are given is on you.

It is your choice. Are you living like your spirit yearns for you to live? Or are you limiting your life by living up to the expectations of others? Do you even know what your gifts are? Do you use them? Do you play it safe? Guess what? You won't ever be able to see the work that God can do through you unless you break through the barriers your soul beckons you to conquer.

When we live in the mold of how others want us to live, we betray our own individuality. You have the choice to break free from that and to use the gifts that God blessed you with. Don't be that person that goes through life like a robot each day. You know what I am talking about.

Take a chance, be thankful, love, create, experience, have faith, and actually LIVE each day of this very precious and finite life you have been given. These precious seconds, minutes, days are truly gifts and blessings that shouldn't be wasted.

It's up to you... now go do it!

It will be health to your flesh, And strength to your bones.

— PROVERBS 3:8, NKJV

There are different kinds of gifts. But it is the same Holy Spirit Who gives them. There are different kinds of work to be done for Him. But the work is for the same Lord. There are different ways of doing His work. But it is the same God who uses all these ways in all people. The Holy Spirit works in each person in one way or another for the good of all. One person is given the gift of teaching words of wisdom. Another person is given the gift of teaching what he has learned and knows. These gifts are by the same Holy Spirit. One person receives the gift of faith. Another person receives the gifts of healing. These gifts are given by the same Holy Spirit. One person is given the gift of doing powerful works. Another person is given the gift of speaking God's Word. Another person is given the gift of telling the difference between the Holy Spirit and false spirits. Another person is given the gift of speaking in special sounds. Another person is given the gift of telling what these special sounds mean. But it is the same Holy Spirit, the Spirit of God, Who does all these things. He gives to each person as He wants to give.

— **1 CORINTHIANS 12:4-11, NLV**

Chapter 58: Fork in the Road

Each of us have these turning points in our lives, these forks in the road that propel us in such a wildly different direction from where we would have gone with our manner of living had we made a different decision. I believe that we have many of these occurrences in our lifetime. Perhaps when they happened, we didn't know how profound each decision was. It may have seemed so simple and mundane at the time. Or conceivably, it was a monumental decision to complexly change who we are because we had become so far away from the authentic self that God had created us to be.

We have so many "forks" within our journeys along the way of our soul paths. It is really interesting sometimes to look back and see just how far one single decision took you.

A decision to...

Change your health, how you eat and how you exercise.

Stop drinking.

Stop smoking.

To love someone.

To take a class.

Turn left versus right.

Have the affair or do something that is wrong when you know it is wrong.

Spend your time a certain way.

Follow God and trust Him.

Have a meeting where an idea was born.

Take a different job.

Apologize.

Have bitterness and not forgive.

Learn an instrument.

To be content with what you have.

To work harder.

To take that interview.

Make that phone call.

I could go on and on.

When I had first moved out to Southern California, I could not find a job. Seriously, no one would hire me. Interview after interview, everyone said, "No." I was starting to get concerned and scared. What the heck was going on?

After one particularly disappointing failed interview, I decided to go to the pool at the apartment complex. It was there I befriended another woman who told me about a party she was going to that night and asked me if I wanted to go. I hesitantly said I would, although that would not be something that I typically did.

While at the party, I overheard another woman tell her friend about how difficult it was to find someone who was useful and not lazy for a position that she had as a receptionist at a mortgage company.

My interview got set up for that Monday. The rest is history. That party changed the entire direction of my life. To think of what would have happened to me had I not gone to that party--where would I be?

Now, I believe that this was God orchestrating, and I just had to be willing and open to let it happen the way it was supposed to happen. The roadblocks in front of me weren't really roadblocks--they were hard stops designed for me to help get me where I was meant to be. I listened to my "gut" (God) and followed on the path that I was supposed to take. I try to imagine what my life would have been like had I not chosen to go to that party.

I also think back to the times that I had my gut feeling, and I ignored it to make a completely different decision. Those choices have never had a great outcome. Never ever.

Your authentic path has been already laid out for you... but you have to make the decision(s) to either follow or not. I believe that we have these "gut feelings" for a reason. Those premonitions that tug on you to do something... you should follow those.

Look back over each day and notice how many times we

are "tugged" in a direction. Look back and see how God was right there with you, trying to help you navigate your way through even the most difficult days.

I know that I have written some deep stuff right there, LOL. It is just neat to think about sometimes--the decisions that we make and just how important they are. Listening to that inner voice that pleads for us to go one way or the other...

> What he opens no one can shut, and what he shuts no one can open.
>
> **— REVELATIONS 3:7, NIV**

> Ask and keep on asking and it will be given to you; seek and keep on seeking and you will find; knock and keep on knocking and the **door** will be opened to you.
>
> **— MATTHEW 7:7, AMP**

> The steps of a [good and righteous] man are directed and established by the Lord, And He delights in his way [and blesses his path].
>
> **— PSALM 37:7, AMP**

Chapter 59: Your Health is Your Wealth

I can hear my Grandma saying it to me now, "Your health is your wealth," and dang it, she is right. Gram is ninety-one, and she is still a firecracker! If you don't have your health, then you have NOTHING... no matter how well off you are:

No health equals no wealth.

You can have all of the money in the world... but if you're sick and can't do anything with it, then you have nothing.

Thanks, Gram!

Most people don't think about how today's actions are going to affect themselves later in life. If you don't take the time to exercise, eat good and nutritious food, and de-stress now, how are you going to feel ten, fifteen, or thirty years from now? Horrible.

You have GOT to take care of yourself. You only get one body. How do you want to be when you get old? Do you want to be fit? Able to do things? Healthy? Take those actions now to ensure that before it is too late. Or don't take any action and see what happens. You won't like it one bit.

We have this amazing ability to make changes in our lives. I am a prime example. Back in my twenties and early thirties, I was unhealthy. I smoked and ate whatever I wanted to. Didn't exercise. Worked eighty-plus hours a week. Ick. I look at pictures of myself from back in those days, and I can hardly even recognize myself. Totally gross. Sometimes, I wonder what I would be like today if I would have stayed on that route that I was on.

Cancer hit me in my early thirties, and I decided to make a change in my life. I started working out almost daily. I stopped drinking pop. I stopped eating processed food whenever I could help it, and my fridge is now full of fresh food. I rarely eat sugar.

And I feel better now at the age of forty-five than I did when I was in my twenties. I FEEL like I look younger too--softer, if that makes sense. I look and feel completely different just by changing my lifestyle. Trust me, it was very difficult when I first started, but now making healthy choices is so easy, and it is just part of my life now.

I don't think that it is ever "too late" to change your lifestyle (unless you are dead). There are no excuses not too stop that destructive path you are on and to get your butt on a new path.

If you are unable to exercise due to a health issue, then you CAN eat right. There is always something that you can do to make your life healthier. Always.

As my wise Grandmother says, "Your health is your wealth." So, what are you waiting for?

Then you will have healing for your body and strength for your bones.

— PROVERBS 3:8, NLT

The Lord nurses them when they are sick and restores them to health.

— PSALM 41:3, NLT

Chapter 60: Being Brave

Lately, I have made it a point to talk to the younger "kids" (that is how I know I am getting older--I call people in their early twenties "kids"). I meet about their goals, aspirations, career choices, and things like that. From these conversations, there has been one common theme that I have heard over and over again:

"I really want to do XXXX, but I am scared of failing."

Or:

"It's my dream to do XXXX, but what if I don't make it?"

So, instead of "going for it," they stay at their current mundane job they hate because they're too scared to follow their dreams for fear of failing. They are perfectly okay with living with their parents while they make minimum wage. It is safe. They still get their participation trophy for *trying* to make it in this world.

Since when is failing a BAD thing? In life, I have learned way, way more from my failures than I have my successes. Failure does not have to be a bad thing. It just means that I tried... and maybe learned that what I once thought I wanted, wasn't really for me. Or I realize that next time when I try a certain thing, I'll do it a little differently. Failing is a GOOD thing. Trust me.

Yeah, it's scary to take that leap of faith doing something you believe you were meant to do, but darn it, kids, you won't know until you try. Yeah, you might fall on your face, but what if you don't? Would you rather live a life of "what if" or a life of "I went for it?"

There are so many people who sit around and reminisce about things that they wish they could do or want to do. Then there are people who DO. Which one do you want to be?

Be BOLD! Stop being afraid to fail.

Fearlessly, just go for it... please!

Follow that inner voice that beckons you and tugs at your spirit. It is there for a reason.

You are fearfully and wonderfully made. You weren't made to blend in, so stand out.

Dear one, it is okay to be scared, but you need to dig inside yourself and put your big girl pants on--at least TRY so that you will know. When you do try, you must try with all of your heart. Don't be half-hearted. Give it all of your effort. I think you'll be surprised at what you have inside of you. Courage that you didn't even know was there. The cool thing is this: once you discover that courage, it will grow... I promise.

Thank you for making me so wonderfully complex!

Being Brave

Your workmanship is marvelous—how well I know it.

— **PSALM 139:14, NLT**

For as these qualities are yours and are increasing [in you as you grow toward spiritual maturity], they will keep you from being useless and unproductive in regard to the true knowledge and greater understanding of our Lord Jesus Christ. For whoever lacks these qualities is blind—shortsighted [closing his spiritual eyes to the truth], having become oblivious to the fact that he was cleansed from his old sins. Therefore, believers, be all the more diligent to make certain about His calling and choosing you [be sure that your behavior reflects and confirms your relationship with God]; for by [a]doing these things [actively developing these virtues], you will never stumble [in your spiritual growth and will live a life that leads others away from sin];

— **2 PETER 1:8-10, AMP**

Chapter 61: Amazing Grace – A Testimony of How God Can Change a Most Broken Man

Sometimes we wonder, *why.*

Why me?

Why did I have to endure so much pain?

Why is this happening to me?

The answers don't always come easy, as you well know. Sometimes it takes many years for them to come... occasionally, they never do. It is up to you.

This story is about the power of God, how He writes His story for your life long before you are born. How there is a reason for your pain, your sorrow, and suffering, and how all of those really messy parts that we see on the outside are all working together for His glory at the end. It is a story of a man who through most of his life was a bit of a mess--to say the least--until he invited God into his life. It is one of the greatest personal testimonies that I have heard.

His name is Michael.

The Storm

The name *Michael* actually means "who is like God." He is one of the archangels. I know that when he was growing up, he didn't feel this way. He rejected God. He hated God.

One of the stories from his childhood is when he and his brothers were little, and they used to sit on the porch on the farm in Iowa waiting for their father to come home from work. One day, he never came back. It was freezing cold outside. One by one, his brothers went back inside, tired of waiting for their father. Michael continued to sit there and wait... and wait... until it got dark and very late. His mother says she carried him inside, and his tears had turned into icicles his eyelashes and cheeks. He later found out that his father no longer wanted the "responsibility" of children, so he just left. Michael was devastated. He felt abandoned. Unloved.

His mother, being newly single, was forced to find a job... any job... and had landed a great one in San Antonio, TX. Although she didn't want to leave the farm, she was forced to for financial reasons. Raising three boys on her own had proven itself to be very challenging, and tough decisions had to be made. Michael was devastated because he was so close to his grandfather and didn't want to leave him. The family packed up its belongings and relocated to Texas, anyway.

He was a sad child. Always wanted attention. He was angry and wanted to be noticed. He explained that he used to do bad things and really didn't know *why* he did them. He just did. Maybe it was the thrill and the possibility of either getting caught or not that enticed him to further act like he did. He was almost looking to be punished. Being a bad kid made him feel good. He wanted to have a reputation where people knew, "not to mess with Mike," and he was recognized accordingly.

Fast forward into high school. Things escalated with his acting out. He was now getting drunk and high every day. He was successful in furthering the reputation that he wanted so badly. He got into fights. He became a thief. His friends weren't much better. He was a mess.

He had become a full-blown alcoholic and a drug addict.

Whenever anyone talked to him about God, he became furious. He felt that all "religious" people were hypocritical and fake. It was all fire and brimstone. He cursed God growing up. He didn't understand how God could let this happen to kids like him. He was convinced that God could and would never love him because of all of the horrible things that he had done in his life, knowing that there was more to come. He was confident in his thoughts and would say, "God, if you don't like me then I don't like YOU. I didn't ASK to be here, so if I make wrong decisions, then I am going to spend eternity in hell? What kind of God does that?"

He felt doomed. The God that he *thought* he knew, oh that God could **never** like him, nevertheless *love* him. Michael felt that no one loved him, not even his mom. He thought that her words were obligatory when she told him that she loved him and something that mom's just *had* to say.

He drank and abused drugs to numb his pain that ached within him. Feeling nothing was better than feeling anything. On the rare days he didn't drink, he would say to himself, "Man, I have got to get my life together" and would stop drinking and doing any drugs out of sheer willpower. He lasted for a month sometimes, at the most. Predictably, he would give in and tell himself that he would just have six drinks. It inevitably ended up being more like eighteen or twenty-four, and when he got drunk enough, he wanted more. He would stop caring, and when that urge started, it would not stop. He was on a mission, and he would do whatever it took to get that next drink or that next drug.

Countless incident after incident, he would wake up the next day feeling like he was a worthless human being. *The biggest loser ever.* His mind would tell him that he would never be able to get his life together, so what was the point?

He thought many times that if he were to die right now, it would be okay. He thought about it many times. How could he keep hurting the people he loved the most? The devil *thought* that he had his hand on Michael.

Then came surrender.

The days before his surrender were like many others. Up for days on end and drunk and high for all of them. His wife had asked him for a divorce, and he knew that this time she meant it.

Michael's thoughts kept on prodding him. "Alright, it is time to stop. Time to ask for help." He had never asked for help before. He had gone to AA many times but always came up with reasons not to like *those AA people.*

This time was different, and he felt it. He was ready to put himself out there and actually get a sponsor. He had never done that before. Instead of just going through the motions, he would fully participate. This time was going to be different. The only potential pitfall was that he didn't believe in the *Greater Power* aspect of the program just yet and the so-called strength behind all of it. He would do all the other parts, though, he told himself.

He took up residence to a small apartment on his boss's land. He didn't have much. His clothes, a Bible that had been a gift, and his Big Blue Book were amongst his few possessions. His divorce was moving forward. He had lost everything.

His living quarters were supposed to have been very temporary, he originally thought. He found out that night that they were not. He was never going back home.

Panic and fury ensued as he practically destroyed his apartment in a rage. He couldn't breathe. He looked at the cabinet where he kept his gun and contemplated death. It would be so easy.

Another thought sprung into his mind. He vividly remembered running up the stairs and then getting onto his knees. He believed that the worst possible thing that could ever happen was befalling him at that moment, and he knew that it was his actions that caused it.

Still angry and in his madness, he yelled, "FINE! FINE! All right, You got me! Do with me what You want!"

And at that moment, a calmness and peace had come over him. He took a deep breath, and it was quiet.

He looked up and wondered what he was to do next. The first thing his eyes came upon was his Big Blue Book. The tranquility that enveloped him after being so frantic affirmed what he was supposed to do.

The subsequent days were much different than before. Mike really started participating in the AA program. He surrounded himself only with people that were positive influences. He started going to church groups. He worked on his relationship with Jesus every day.

This time, he earnestly *and* honestly went through the Twelve Steps. It was hard work and took a LOT of self-searching that he didn't like much at times. Some steps took three-four months to complete. All twelve took him the entire year. He took his time, and he was good with it.

Michael's mother would call him every morning and pray with and for him on the way to work. Gone were the gratuitous absences and excuses of his old days. The "new Michael" went to work every day without fail.

Most importantly, God had taken the desire of drinking and drugs away from Michael. He also provided him with good friends... actually, the best friends that he had ever had. Mike had no inclination to hang out with his old crew because he was now a follower of Christ. His new friends provided love and encouragement, as true friends should.

The comfort and serenity that he had searched for his whole life were now right in front of him. He *felt* it. That was another thing. It had been so long since he had actually *felt* something. Hurt, joy, sorrow, excitement, nervousness, love, responsibility.... all of these "new" feelings overwhelmed him.

He wanted to experience everything that this newfound life had to offer. He wanted to *feel* because he had led a numbed life for so long. Now that he was a follower of Christ, he knew that he had to be a different man. He felt he had one shot, and he was "done being a loser."

And he was.

He started taking better care of his body. He exercised and got enough sleep. Michael's drive for success became more and more fueled. He bought a house on his own. Huge victory.

Now what?

Before his total immersion into the program and his complete surrender to God, he would go to AA meetings and listen to *other* men talk about how they used to be. He would see them drive up in their fancy cars and hear about their successful businesses and think to himself, "That only happens to other people, not me."

God kept on urging him to start his own business and go off on his own but fear still had a grip on him. He knew deep down that he could be successful, but he needed the courage to make his move. He listened to the Christian song "Voice of Truth"[2] for about six months--over and over, every single day. That song gave him the audacity to begin his progression into making that leap he had long dreamed about.

His desire to become self-employed was propelled quickly because the company that he had been working for during the past ten years announced, suddenly, that they were going out of business. Time to jump. God's timing was perfect.

Now, Mike is, one of those guys who talks about how he used to be. He is a changed man.

There's a lot we can all takeaway from this story.

It doesn't matter where you come from or what you have done. God loves you and can transform you from the inside out. He forgives. He redeems. He remolds.

You ask, "Why?"

And God answers, "To show others my power through your testimony. To bring others to Me." Without a test, there is no testimony, right?

"Why did this happen to me?"

"To bring you closer to Me," God whispers.

"Why must I have pain?"

"To show you My grace," He says. "Without your pain, you would not feel this joy and peace."

I believe that everything that happened in Michael's life led him to be right where God wanted him to be. It was already in His plan. Michael just had to surrender. The man of God that he has become is a perfect conformation of what man can do *with* God.

Our hope. Our rock. Our salvation. Our fortress.

He wants us to pour out our hearts to Him. Trust Him. Seek Him, and turn our gaze to Him. Wait for Him in the silence that comes between your thoughts. He is there. Waiting.

Amazing grace
How sweet the sound
That saved a wretch like me
I once was lost
But now I'm found
Was blind, but now I see
'Twas grace that taught
My heart to fear
And grace my Fears relieved
How precious did
That grace appear

The Storm

The hour I first believed

Through many dangers

Toils and snares

We have already come

'Twas grace hath brought

Us safe thus far

And grace will lead us home

When we've been there

Ten thousand years

Bright shining as the sun

We'll have no less days to sing God's praise

Than when we first begun

Amazing grace

How sweet the sound

That saved a wretch like me

I once was lost

But now I'm found

Was blind, but now I see.[3]

Chapter 62: I Can't Do This!

I can't do this. This is too hard. I can't do this. It is too much for me to deal with. I can't do this.

Ever feel this way? You're right at the time you have these thoughts. *You can't.*

Want to know why? Because you forgot a very important word at the end--*alone*.

When you say, "I can't do this," you're right, and when you say, "I can't do this alone," you're also right.

My question to you though is this: which one is better? Which one do you want to believe?

Sure, by your own strength, your own courage, your own will - you *can't* do this. You can't get through it. Sure, you might be fine for a little while, but it won't last. You aren't strong enough. It's okay.

Oh, with God though, you CAN--and you will. He gives supernatural powers to overcome and conquer our most daunting challenges. God boosts our courage, tenacity, will, love, peace, and understanding of our situations. He heals the sick. Comforts the weak. Takes our burdens. He's our rock and our refuge. Our reward.

The Storm

He transforms His children into mighty warriors.

So, next time the devil whispers in your ear, "You can't do this," do this.

Shout right back to him, "I know I can't... by myself. With God I can. So back the heck off, slimeball, 'cause God is right here with me. He will fight for me and protect me. He is my strength. He will provide. He will give me peace and He loves me."

You are my hiding place;

you will protect me from trouble

and surround me with songs of deliverance.

—PSALM 32:7, NIV

Be strong and courageous. Do not be afraid or terrified because of them, for the Lord your God goes with you; he will never leave you nor forsake you.

— DEUTERONOMY 32:6, NIV

I keep my eyes always on the Lord.

With him at my right hand, I will not be shaken.

— PSALM 16:8, NIV

Chapter 63: A Prayer for Healing

I get it. You feel like you've been dealt a bad hand. The storm in your life is hard to deal with. Your overwhelming feelings are exhausting.

When things like this happen, we have choices, right? We can get really resentful and aggrieved. We can shake our fists in the air and scream, "Why me?" We can sink into a deep depression and sulk. We can have a pity party for ourselves and spend the rest of our lives using our illness or circumstance as an excuse not to live.

Or...

We can fight. We can believe and have faith that God is going to give us one heck of a testimony for healing or strength or both. We can NOT just give up and accept our circumstances as a justification or a cop-out for not enjoying each beautiful moment that we have been given.

We need to believe that we will be healed... and if we are not, it just means that God has a better plan for us. One that we just can't see yet.

God will use us to help people. God will use us so He can show people what miracles can happen because He is with us.

We have to keep a positive attitude. We have to continue to have a healthy lifestyle. We have to take very good care of ourselves both physically and mentally. We need to be present in our moments and continue to value those around us. We have to *live* our lives.

Now is also a good time to ask a question that maybe you have never asked. *What is the Holy Spirit wanting you to do with this time?* I pray that you ask Him to open your heart and tell you what He wants you to do. People will know that your life was changed because of the supernatural power that you have along with the Holy Spirit. There will be no other explanation for it.

It won't be easy, but don't be scared. We know that we are not alone. God is just getting started with what He is doing with you.

Maybe your miracle is that you will inspire others around you and bring them to God. Maybe your miracle is extravagant love that you are able to receive or give. Perhaps it will be a mended relationship. Quite possibly, your miracle is complete healing.

Regardless, you *will* have a miracle. Maybe not the one you expect, but you know how God is--He has His plan. His are way better than ours. He knows what He is doing.

First, you have to believe it will happen. Second, you have to have faith in God and trust that He will bring you through this storm. Third, you have to have your heart wide open. You have to be able to hear the whispers and believe them with all that you have. You have to be ready to receive.

Here is my prayer for you, using God's words to guide you through it.

Mighty Father, today I come to You because now, more than I ever have, I need You. I'm not afraid because I know that You are with me. You heal the brokenhearted, and You will bind my wounds. I humble myself before You, Lord. I am seeking Your face, Mighty Lord, and I am praying that You hear me from heaven. Please forgive my sins and heal me.

I ask for the sun of righteousness to rise and heal me with its rays. Heal me, Lord, and I will be healed. Save me, Lord, and I will be saved. I praise You with all of my heart and all of my soul--everything within me praises You, my savior. I love You in that same way too. My burden right now is so heavy that I cannot carry it anymore myself. Please take this anxiety from my heart and cast off the troubles of my body. Create in me a pure heart, O God, and renew a steadfast spirit within me.

I trust You, Lord, with all of my heart, and I will not lean unto my own understanding. I submit my ways to You. I trust in Your unfailing love and my heart rejoices in Your salvation. I will sing your praise, for You have been so good to me.

The Storm

Let me rest beside You, Lord, while I am in my deep valley. I know that Your mercy and goodness will follow me all of the days of my life, and that I will dwell in Your house for eternity.

No matter what happens to me, Lord, I know that there is a reason for it, far greater than I will understand. I accept that. When I go to sleep at night, I know that it is You who keeps me safe.

Show me the way that I should go. I entrust my life to You. I feel like I am blind right now because I can't see the purpose in all of this, but I know that You do. So, I will wait for You. You are my refuge in my times of trouble. You are my strength and my shield. My heart is leaping for joy right now because I know You are listening to me.

When I awake in the morning, I know that You are right there with me--my light and my salvation. What do I have to fear? I have You as my stronghold.

You know everything about me, God. You know the hairs on my head, and You know everything that I do. Your strength will always support me, and Your light will always show me the way. You knew what my life would be like before I was ever born, and You love me as Your precious child. Thank You, dear God. Thank You.

So guide me, dear Lord. In you, I have peace. Your love

protects, gives me hope, and always perseveres.

Thank You for Your miracles. Thank You for Your healing. Thank You for the wonderful life that You have given me. I love You, Lord.

Amen

Chapter 64: A Journal for Overcoming

You might not think this now, but the tough times you're going through right now will shape you. The choice that you have to make is what shape do you want to be? You can come out of this better and stronger than you were, or you can accept defeat and give up. It is up to you.

Take some time to think and journal about the questions I pose to you. They will help you grow into who God has meant for you to be.

Think about all of the adversities in your life that you have *already* overcome. List out some of your major life occurrences. Write about what you initially felt when you were going through them and then about what you think of them now. Focus specifically on what you were like as a person before and after.

_____

_____

_____

_____

_____

_____

_____

_____

_____

_____

_____

_____

_____

_____

_____

_____

_____

_____

_____

Now that you have thought about those, journal about how you are going to handle your tough times differently this time.

_____

_____

_____

_____

_____

_____

_____

_____

A Journal for Overcoming

When you are at your weakest moments, the best thing that you can do is to get on your knees and talk to God. Write a prayer to Him now and earnestly pray it.

_____

_____

_____

_____

_____

_____

_____

_____

_____

_____

_____

_____

_____

_____

_____

_____

_____

How does God's strength show through your weakness?

_____

_____

_____

The Storm

_____

_____

_____

_____

In order to overcome, you have to work on your recovery every single day. What steps are you taking to help and heal yourself?

_____

_____

_____

_____

_____

_____

_____

_____

_____

_____

_____

_____

Have you even been in denial about something that is wrong with you? Why were you? Would you ever ignore your body's warning signs again?

_____

_____

A Journal for Overcoming

_____
_____
_____
_____

What is your gameplay for your long-term recovery?

_____
_____
_____
_____
_____
_____
_____

How can you use your current "down time" wisely?

_____
_____
_____
_____
_____
_____

Pray. Pray for God's guidance on what He wants you to do with this precious time. What is He saying?

_____
_____

_____
_____
_____
_____
_____
_____
_____
_____
_____
_____

I get it. You are out of your usual "comfort zone." Now is the time to decide who you want to be and how you are going to react to your life change. Write it out.

_____
_____
_____
_____
_____
_____
_____
_____
_____
_____
_____
_____
_____

A Journal for Overcoming

_____
_____
_____
_____
_____
_____
_____
_____
_____
_____
_____
_____
_____

What is the devil trying to whisper in your ear?

_____
_____
_____
_____
_____
_____

What are you telling him right back?

_____
_____
_____

_____

_____

_____

_____

Write a letter to God thanking Him for the good things in your life. Be specific.

_____

_____

_____

_____

_____

_____

_____

_____

_____

_____

_____

_____

_____

_____

_____

_____

_____

_____

_____

_____

_____
_____
_____
_____
_____
_____
_____

How has pruning made you a stronger person?

_____
_____
_____
_____
_____
_____

God tells us over and over that we are never alone. How does that statement impact how you react to your "negative" situation?

_____
_____
_____
_____
_____
_____

The Storm

God arms us with His protection. Facing your problems head on becomes easier when we have God with us. Thank the Lord right now for His everlasting love. Think about what this battle would be like if you didn't have a relationship with Him.

_____

_____

_____

_____

_____

_____

_____

_____

_____

_____

_____

How do you know that everything is going to be okay?

_____

_____

_____

_____

_____

_____

A Journal for Overcoming

How have your scars made you who you are?

_____

_____

_____

_____

_____

_____

_____

_____

_____

How have the days that you have lived shaped who you are today?

_____

_____

_____

_____

_____

_____

_____

_____

_____

_____

_____

_____

_____

The Storm

If you were to die today, would you have regrets about not living the life you should have had?

_____
_____
_____
_____
_____
_____
_____

Why haven't you started living <u>that</u> life?

_____
_____
_____
_____
_____
_____
_____

What are some dreams that you have had but haven't done them yet? Name five.

_____
_____
_____
_____
_____
_____

_____

_____

Do you feel like you have lived a life un-lived? Have you lived the best life that you could? What can you do to change things if you have not lived to your full potential?

_____

_____

_____

_____

_____

_____

What are some decisions that you have made in your past that propelled you wildly in a certain direction?

_____

_____

_____

_____

_____

_____

_____

_____

_____

_____

_____

_____

What decision(s) can you make today that will dramatically change your life?

_____

_____

_____

_____

_____

_____

_____

Are you taking as good of care of your body as you can right now?

_____

_____

_____

_____

What one thing can you do right now that would improve your health?

_____

_____

_____

_____

_____

Name five "failures" that you have had and what you
have learned from them.

_____

_____

_____

_____

_____

_____

_____

_____

_____

_____

_____

_____

_____

_____

What GOOD things came out of them?

_____

_____

The Storm

_____

_____

_____

_____

_____

_____

_____

_____

_____

_____

What do you want to do but have not had the courage?

_____

_____

_____

_____

_____

_____

What is the worst thing that could happen if you did it?

_____

_____

_____

_____

_____

A Journal for Overcoming

What is stopping you? What are you afraid of?

_____

_____

_____

_____

_____

_____

_____

Your past does not dictate your future. Write about some ways you have overcome some bad things from your childhood or your past.

_____

_____

_____

_____

_____

_____

_____

_____

_____

Write your testimony.

_____

_____

_____

The Storm

_____

_____

_____

_____

_____

_____

_____

_____

_____

_____

_____

_____

_____

_____

_____

_____

_____

_____

_____

When you surrender yourself completely to Jesus, the way that you suffer through your trials changes. What is the biggest change you have noticed?

_____

_____

_____

_____

_____

_____

_____

Which is better: going through your difficult time by yourself or with God?

_____

_____

_____

_____

_____

_____

_____

In what ways can you use your struggles to help inspire others?

_____

_____

_____

_____

_____

_____

_____

_____

_____

_____

_____

_____

What do you think <u>your</u> miracle is?

_____

_____

_____

_____

_____

_____

_____

Why is it so important for you to keep a positive attitude?

_____

_____

_____

_____

_____

_____

What is the Holy Spirit wanting you to do at this time? If the answer is not clear, pray to the Holy Spirit for guidance. Write down what your soul feels.

_____

_____

_____

The Storm

_____

_____

_____

_____

_____

_____

_____

_____

_____

How are you going to live your life differently once your storm is over?

_____

_____

_____

_____

_____

_____

_____

_____

_____

_____

_____

_____

_____

Epilogue

I want you to breathe a little with me for a few minutes. Slow, deep breaths.

Inhale...forgiveness.

Exhale...your fear.

Inhale...peace.

Exhale...anxiety.

Inhale...love.

Exhale...resentment.

Listen for God's voice in your life. His love is unconditional. Unfailing. Unfathomable.

He is right there with you, and when you reach out your arms to accept Him, He comes running into them.

If there is any unforgiveness in you, pray that He helps you release it. Love others like He loves you.

If there is a relationship that needs to mended, an apology that needs to be done, or anything else that the Holy Spirit is nudging you to do--do it now.

Confess your sins and make things right with Him and those around you. You, my dear friend, are God's child, and nothing can separate you from Him.

Jen

Endnotes

[1] St. Patrick, "The Deer's Cry," Unknown Publisher. Translated by Kuno Meyer, 1920.

2.Casting Crowns, "Voice of Truth," track 3 on *Casting Crowns*, Beach Street, 2003, compact disc.

3. John Newton, "Amazing Grace," (Christian Hymn: 1779), https://en.wikipedia.org/wiki/Amazing_Grace

CPSIA information can be obtained
at www.ICGtesting.com
Printed in the USA
LVHW011623260921
698753LV00016B/780

9 781637 693728